FAVORITE BRAND NAME RECIPES

CHRISTMAS COOKIES

From Your Favorite Brand Name Companies

Duncan Hines® ® BORDEN® HERSHEY'S® and many more

Manufactured in U.S.A.

Some of the products listed in this publication may be in limited distribution.

BUTTER FLAVOR CRISCO® is artificially flavored.

Front cover photography by Sanders Studios, Inc., Chicago.

ISBN: 0-7853-1415-6

CHRISTMAS COOKIES

Holiday Favorites

These cookies are sure to bring back delightful holiday memories. Make a batch and start a holiday tradition for your family.

CHOCO-COCO PECAN CRISPS

- **½ cup butter or margarine, softened**
- **1 cup packed light brown sugar**
- **1 egg**
- **1 teaspoon vanilla**
- **1½ cups all-purpose flour**
- **1 cup chopped pecans**
- **⅓ cup unsweetened cocoa**
- **½ teaspoon baking soda**
- **1 cup flaked coconut**

Cream butter and sugar in large bowl until light and fluffy. Beat in egg and vanilla. Combine flour, pecans, cocoa and baking soda in small bowl until well blended. Add to creamed mixture, blending until stiff dough is formed. Sprinkle coconut on work surface. Divide dough into 4 parts. Shape each part into a roll, about 1½ inches in diameter; roll in coconut until thickly coated. Wrap in plastic wrap; chill until firm, at least 1 hour or up to 2 weeks. (For longer storage, freeze up to 6 weeks.)

Preheat oven to 350°F. Line cookie sheets with parchment paper or leave ungreased. Cut rolls into ⅛-inch-thick slices. Place 2 inches apart on cookie sheets.

Bake 10 to 13 minutes or until firm, but not overly browned. Remove to wire racks to cool.

Makes about 6 dozen cookies

***Left:** Choco-Coco Pecan Crisps*
***Right:** Holiday Fruit Drops (page 4)*

HOLIDAY FRUIT DROPS

1/2 cup butter, softened
3/4 cup packed brown sugar
1 egg
1 1/4 cups all-purpose flour
1 teaspoon vanilla
1/2 teaspoon baking soda
1/2 teaspoon ground cinnamon
Pinch salt
1 cup (8 ounces) diced candied pineapple
1 cup (8 ounces) red and green candied cherries
8 ounces chopped pitted dates
1 cup (6 ounces) semisweet chocolate chips
1/2 cup whole hazelnuts
1/2 cup pecan halves
1/2 cup coarsely chopped walnuts

Preheat oven to 325°F. Lightly grease cookie sheets or line with parchment paper. Cream butter and sugar in large bowl. Beat in egg until light. Mix in flour, vanilla, baking soda, cinnamon and salt. Stir in pineapple, cherries, dates, chocolate chips, hazelnuts, pecans and walnuts. Drop dough by rounded teaspoonfuls 2 inches apart onto prepared cookie sheets.

Bake 15 to 20 minutes or until firm and lightly browned around edges. Remove to wire racks to cool completely.

Makes about 8 dozen cookies

Note: The cherries, hazelnuts and pecans are not chopped, but left whole.

CHOCOLATE-DIPPED OAT COOKIES

2 cups uncooked rolled oats
3/4 cup packed brown sugar
1/2 cup vegetable oil
1/2 cup finely chopped walnuts
1 egg
2 teaspoons grated orange peel
1/4 teaspoon salt
1 package (11 1/2 ounces) milk chocolate chips

Combine oats, sugar, oil, walnuts, egg, orange peel and salt in large bowl until blended. Cover; refrigerate overnight.

Preheat oven to 350°F. Lightly grease cookie sheets or line with parchment paper. Melt chocolate chips in top of double boiler over hot, not boiling, water; set aside. Shape oat mixture into large marble-sized balls. Place 2 inches apart on prepared cookie sheets.

Bake 10 to 12 minutes or until golden and crisp. Cool 10 minutes on wire racks. Dip tops of cookies, one at a time, into melted chocolate. Place on waxed paper; cool until chocolate is set.

Makes about 6 dozen cookies

LEMON BLOSSOM COOKIES

2 cups margarine or butter, softened
1½ cups confectioners' sugar
¼ cup REALEMON® Lemon Juice from Concentrate
4 cups unsifted all-purpose flour
Finely chopped nuts (optional)
Assorted fruit preserves and jams or pecan halves

In large mixer bowl, beat margarine and sugar until fluffy. Add ReaLemon® brand; beat well. Gradually add flour; mix well. Cover and chill 2 hours.

Preheat oven to 350°F. Grease cookie sheets. Shape dough into 1-inch balls; roll in nuts, if desired. Place 1 inch apart on prepared cookie sheets. Press thumb in center of each ball; fill with preserves or pecan half.

Bake 14 to 16 minutes or until lightly browned. Remove to wire rack to cool completely. *Makes about 6 dozen cookies*

EUROPEAN KOLACKY

1 cup butter or margarine, softened
1 package (8 ounces) cream cheese, softened
1 tablespoon milk
1 tablespoon sugar
1 egg yolk
1½ cups all-purpose flour
½ teaspoon baking powder
1 can SOLO® or 1 jar BAKER® Filling (any flavor)
Confectioners' sugar

Beat butter, cream cheese, milk and sugar in medium bowl with electric mixer until thoroughly blended. Beat in egg yolk. Sift together flour and baking powder; stir into butter mixture to make stiff dough. Cover and refrigerate several hours or overnight.

Preheat oven to 400°F. Roll out dough on lightly floured surface to ¼-inch thickness. Cut dough with floured 2-inch cookie cutter. Place cookies on ungreased cookie sheets about 1 inch apart. Make depression in centers of cookies with thumb or back of spoon. Spoon 1 teaspoon filling into centers of cookies.

Bake 10 to 12 minutes or until lightly browned. Remove from baking sheets and cool completely on wire racks. Sprinkle with confectioners' sugar just before serving. *Makes about 3 dozen cookies*

APRICOT-PECAN TASSIES

BASE
1 cup all-purpose flour
1/2 cup butter, cut into pieces
6 tablespoons reduced-calorie cream cheese

FILLING
3/4 cup firmly packed light brown sugar
1 egg, lightly beaten
1 tablespoon butter, softened
1/2 teaspoon vanilla
1/4 teaspoon salt
2/3 cup California dried apricot halves, diced (about 4 ounces)
1/3 cup chopped pecans

For base, in food processor, combine flour, 1/2 cup butter and cream cheese; process until mixture forms large ball. Wrap dough in plastic wrap and chill 15 minutes.

For filling, combine brown sugar, egg, 1 tablespoon butter, vanilla and salt in bowl until smooth. Stir in apricots and nuts.

Preheat oven to 325°F. Shape dough into 2 dozen 1-inch balls and place in paper-lined or greased miniature muffin cups. Press dough on bottom and up side of each cup; fill each with 1 teaspoon apricot-pecan filling. Bake 25 minutes or until golden and filling sets. Cool and remove from cups. Cookies can be wrapped tightly in plastic and frozen up to six weeks. *Makes 2 dozen cookies*

Favorite recipe from California Apricot Advisory Board

SNOWBALLS

1/2 cup DOMINO® Confectioners 10-X Sugar
1/4 teaspoon salt
1 cup butter or margarine, softened
1 teaspoon vanilla extract
2 1/4 cups all-purpose flour
1/2 cup chopped pecans
Additional DOMINO® Confectioners 10-X Sugar

In large bowl, combine 1/2 cup sugar, salt and butter; mix well. Add vanilla. Gradually stir in flour. Work nuts into dough. Cover and chill until firm.

Preheat oven to 400°F. Form dough into 1-inch balls. Place 1 inch apart on ungreased cookie sheets. Bake 8 to 10 minutes or until set, but not brown. Roll in additional sugar immediately. Cool on wire racks. Roll in sugar again. Store in airtight container. *Makes about 5 dozen cookies*

Apricot-Pecan Tassies

Chocolate-Dipped Almond Horns

CHOCOLATE-DIPPED ALMOND HORNS

1 can SOLO® Almond Paste
3 egg whites
½ cup superfine sugar
½ teaspoon almond extract
¼ cup plus 2 tablespoons all-purpose flour
½ cup sliced almonds
5 squares (1 ounce each) semisweet chocolate, melted and cooled

Preheat oven to 350°F. Grease 2 cookie sheets; set aside. Break almond paste into small pieces and place in medium bowl or container of food processor. Add egg whites, sugar and almond extract. Beat with electric mixer or process until mixture is very smooth. Add flour and beat or process until blended.

Spoon almond mixture into pastry bag fitted with ½-inch (#8) plain tip. Pipe mixture into 5- or 6-inch crescent shapes on prepared cookie sheets about 1½ inches apart. Sprinkle with sliced almonds.

Bake 13 to 15 minutes or until edges are golden. Cool on cookie sheets on wire racks 2 minutes. Remove from cookie sheets and cool completely on wire racks. Dip ends of cookies in melted chocolate and place on sheet of foil. Let stand until chocolate is set. *Makes about 16 cookies*

SPRITZ

1 BUTTER FLAVOR CRISCO® Stick or 1 cup BUTTER FLAVOR CRISCO all-vegetable shortening
½ cup sugar
1 egg
¾ teaspoon salt
¾ teaspoon vanilla
½ teaspoon almond extract
2¼ cups all-purpose flour

1. Preheat oven to 400°F. Combine shortening and sugar in large bowl. Beat at medium speed of electric mixer until well blended. Beat in egg, salt, vanilla and almond extract. Stir in flour. If dough is too stiff, add a little water. If too soft, add a little extra flour.

2. Place dough in cookie press. Press into desired shapes 2 inches apart on cooled, ungreased baking sheet.

3. Bake 5 to 7 minutes or until set, but not brown. Cool 1 minute. Remove to wire racks to cool completely. *Makes about 4 dozen cookies*

Note: Dough may be tinted using a few drops of food color. Cookies may be iced and decorated, if desired.

ALMOND RASPBERRY MACAROONS

Macaroons are a classic favorite. Here, the deliciously intense flavor of almond paste is punctuated by a dot of raspberry jam.

2 cups BLUE DIAMOND® Blanched Almond Paste
1 cup granulated sugar
6 large egg whites
Powdered sugar
Seedless raspberry jam, stirred until smooth

Preheat oven to 350°F. Line cookie sheets with parchment paper or waxed paper. Beat almond paste and granulated sugar until mixture resembles coarse cornmeal. Beat in egg whites, a little at a time, until thoroughly combined.

Place heaping teaspoonfuls 2 inches apart onto prepared cookie sheets. Coat finger with powdered sugar and make an indentation in middle of each cookie. (Coat finger with powdered sugar each time.)

Bake 15 to 20 minutes or until lightly browned. Remove from oven and fill each indentation with about ¼ teaspoon raspberry jam. Cool. If using waxed paper, carefully peel paper off cookies when cooled.
Makes about 2½ dozen cookies

LEMONY SPRITZ STICKS

1 cup margarine or butter, softened
1 cup confectioners' sugar
¼ cup REALEMON® Lemon Juice from Concentrate
2½ cups unsifted all-purpose flour
¼ teaspoon salt
Chocolate Glaze (recipe follows)
Finely chopped nuts

Preheat oven to 375°F. Grease cookie sheets. In large bowl, beat margarine and sugar until fluffy. Add ReaLemon® brand; beat well. Stir in flour and salt; mix well.

Place dough in cookie press with star-shaped plate. Press dough into 3-inch strips onto prepared cookie sheets. Bake 5 to 6 minutes or until lightly browned on ends. Cool 1 to 2 minutes on cookie sheets. Remove to wire rack to cool completely. Dip ends of cookies in Chocolate Glaze, then nuts. *Makes about 8½ dozen cookies*

Tip: When using electric cookie gun, use decorator tip. Press dough into ½ × 3-inch strips onto greased cookie sheets. Bake 8 to 10 minutes or until lightly browned on ends.

Chocolate Glaze: In small saucepan, melt 3 ounces sweet cooking chocolate and 2 tablespoons margarine or butter. *Makes about ⅓ cup*

SLICE 'N' BAKE PUMPKIN COOKIES

3 cups all-purpose flour
1 tablespoon pumpkin pie spice
2 teaspoons ground ginger
½ teaspoon salt
1 cup butter, softened
2 cups granulated sugar
1 cup LIBBY'S® Solid Pack Pumpkin
1 egg yolk

In medium bowl, combine flour, pumpkin pie spice, ginger and salt; set aside. In large mixer bowl, cream butter and sugar, beating until light and fluffy. Add pumpkin and egg yolk; mix well. Blend in dry ingredients; mix well. Cover and chill until firm. Divide into 4 parts. Place each part on 14×10-inch sheet of plastic wrap. Wrap loosely around dough. Shape into 1½-inch-diameter roll; wrap securely. Freeze 4 hours or until firm.

Preheat oven to 350°F. Grease cookie sheets. Cut rolls into ¼-inch slices. Place 2 inches apart on prepared cookie sheets; pat to spread slightly. Reserve some slices to make pumpkin stems; cut into fourths. Shape and press onto tops of cookie slices to form stems.

Continued

Bake 16 to 18 minutes or until lightly browned. Remove to wire racks to cool completely. Decorate in pumpkin design with orange and green frosting, if desired. *Makes about 5 dozen cookies*

Hint: Spread orange frosting with small spatula. Pipe leaves using leaf frosting tip, then vines with smallest frosting tip.

BAVARIAN COOKIE WREATHS

Use various decorations for special holidays—or serve plain.

3½ cups all-purpose flour
1 cup sugar, divided
3 teaspoons grated orange peel, divided
¼ teaspoon salt
1⅓ cups butter or margarine
¼ cup Florida orange juice
⅓ cup finely chopped blanched almonds
1 egg white beaten *with* 1 teaspoon water
Tinted Frosting (recipe follows)

Preheat oven to 400°F. Lightly grease cookie sheets. In large bowl, mix flour, ¾ cup sugar, 2 teaspoons orange peel and salt. Using pastry blender, cut in butter until mixture resembles coarse crumbs; add orange juice, stirring until mixture holds together. Knead a few times and press into a ball.

Shape dough into ¾-inch balls; lightly roll each on floured surface into 6-inch-long strip. Using two strips, twist together to make rope. Pinch ends of rope together to make wreath; place on prepared cookie sheet.

In shallow dish, mix almonds, remaining ¼ cup sugar and 1 teaspoon orange peel. Brush top of wreaths with egg white mixture and sprinkle with almond-sugar mixture. Bake 8 to 10 minutes or until lightly browned. Remove to wire racks to cool completely. Frost, if desired.
Makes about 5 dozen cookies

TINTED FROSTING

1 cup confectioners' sugar
2 tablespoons butter or margarine, softened
1 to 2 teaspoons milk
Few drops green food color
Red cinnamon candies

In small bowl, mix sugar, butter, 1 teaspoon milk and few drops green food color. Add more milk if necessary to make frosting spreadable. Fill pastry bag fitted with small leaf tip (#67). Decorate each wreath with 3 or 4 leaves and red-cinnamon-candy berries.

Favorite recipe from Florida Department of Citrus

PEANUT BUTTER CHOCOLATE BARS

½ cup (1 stick) margarine, softened
⅓ cup sugar
½ cup QUAKER® or AUNT JEMIMA® Enriched Corn Meal
½ cup all-purpose flour
½ cup chopped almonds
½ cup peanut butter
¼ cup semi-sweet chocolate pieces
1 teaspoon shortening

Preheat oven to 375°F. Beat margarine and sugar until fluffy. Stir in corn meal, flour and almonds. Press onto bottom of ungreased 9-inch square baking pan.

Bake 25 to 30 minutes or until edges are light golden brown. Cool about 10 minutes; spread with peanut butter. In saucepan over low heat, melt chocolate pieces and shortening, stirring until smooth.* Drizzle over peanut butter. Cool completely in pan on wire rack. Cut into bars. Store tightly covered. *Makes 16 bars*

*Microwave directions: Place chocolate pieces and shortening in microwaveable bowl. Microwave at HIGH 1 to 1½ minutes, stirring after 1 minute and then every 15 seconds until smooth.

CHOCOLATE RASPBERRY THUMBPRINTS

1½ cups butter or margarine, softened
1 cup sugar
1 egg
1 teaspoon vanilla extract
3 cups all-purpose flour
¼ cup unsweetened cocoa
½ teaspoon salt
1 cup (6 ounces) semisweet mini chocolate chips
⅔ cup raspberry preserves
Powdered sugar (optional)

Preheat oven to 350°F. Grease cookie sheets. Beat butter and sugar in large bowl. Beat in egg and vanilla until light and fluffy. Mix in flour, cocoa and salt until well blended. Stir in chocolate chips. Roll level tablespoonfuls of dough into balls. Place 2 inches apart onto prepared cookie sheets. Make deep indentation in center of each ball with thumb.

Bake 12 to 15 minutes until just set. Cool 2 minutes on cookie sheets. Remove to wire racks; cool completely. Fill centers with raspberry preserves and sprinkle with powdered sugar, if desired. Store between layers of waxed paper in airtight containers.

Makes about 4½ dozen cookies

CRISPY NUT SHORTBREAD

6 tablespoons margarine, softened
1/3 cup sugar
1 egg
1 teaspoon vanilla
1/2 cup QUAKER® or AUNT JEMIMA® Enriched Corn Meal
1/2 cup all-purpose flour
1/2 cup finely chopped, husked, toasted hazelnuts or walnuts
1/2 cup semi-sweet chocolate pieces
1 tablespoon vegetable shortening
Coarsely chopped nuts (optional)

Preheat oven to 300°F. Grease 13×9-inch baking pan. Beat margarine and sugar until fluffy. Blend in egg and vanilla. Add combined corn meal, flour and nuts; mix well. Spread onto bottom of prepared pan. Bake 40 to 45 minutes or until edges are golden brown.

In saucepan over low heat, melt chocolate pieces and shortening, stirring until smooth.* Spread over shortbread. Sprinkle with coarsely chopped nuts, if desired. Cool completely. Cut into 48 squares; cut diagonally into triangles. Store tightly covered. *Makes 4 dozen cookies*

*Microwave directions: Place chocolate pieces and shortening in microwaveable bowl. Microwave at HIGH 1 to 2 minutes, stirring after 1 minute and then every 30 seconds until smooth.

Crispy Nut Shortbread;
Peanut Butter Chocolate Bars (page 12)

PEANUT BUTTER CRACKLES

- **1½ cups all-purpose flour**
- **1 teaspoon baking soda**
- **⅛ teaspoon salt**
- **½ cup MAZOLA® Margarine, softened**
- **½ cup SKIPPY® Creamy or Super Chunk Peanut Butter**
- **½ cup granulated sugar**
- **½ cup packed brown sugar**
- **1 egg**
- **1 teaspoon vanilla**
- **Granulated sugar**
- **Chocolate candy stars**

Preheat oven to 375°F. In small bowl, combine flour, baking soda and salt. In large bowl, beat margarine and peanut butter until well blended. Beat in granulated sugar and brown sugar until blended. Beat in egg and vanilla. Gradually beat in flour mixture until well mixed.

Shape dough into 1-inch balls. Roll in granulated sugar. Place 2 inches apart on ungreased cookie sheets.

Bake 10 minutes or until lightly browned. Remove from oven and quickly press chocolate star firmly into top of each cookie (cookie will crack around edges). Remove to wire racks to cool completely.

Makes about 5 dozen cookies

JINGLE JUMBLES

- **¾ cup butter or margarine, softened**
- **1 cup packed brown sugar**
- **¼ cup molasses**
- **1 egg**
- **2¼ cups unsifted all-purpose flour**
- **2 teaspoons baking soda**
- **1 teaspoon ground ginger**
- **1 teaspoon ground cinnamon**
- **½ teaspoon salt**
- **½ teaspoon ground cloves**
- **1¼ cups SUN-MAID® Raisins**
- **Granulated sugar**

In large bowl, cream butter and sugar. Add molasses and egg; beat until fluffy. In medium bowl, sift together flour, baking soda, ginger, cinnamon, salt and cloves. Stir into molasses mixture. Stir in raisins. Cover and chill about 30 minutes.

Preheat oven to 375°F. Grease cookie sheets. Form dough into 1½-inch balls; roll in granulated sugar, coating generously. Place 2 inches apart on prepared cookie sheets.

Bake 12 to 14 minutes or until edges are firm and centers are still slightly soft. Remove to wire rack to cool. *Makes about 2 dozen cookies*

Holiday Citrus Logs

HOLIDAY CITRUS LOGS

1 (12-ounce) package vanilla wafers, crushed (about 3 cups)
1 (8-ounce) package candied cherries, coarsely chopped
1 (8-ounce) package chopped dates (1³/₄ cups)
1 cup chopped pecans or almonds
¹/₄ cup REALEMON® Lemon Juice from Concentrate
2 tablespoons orange-flavored liqueur
1 tablespoon white corn syrup
Additional white corn syrup, heated
Additional finely chopped pecans or sliced almonds, toasted

In large bowl, combine all ingredients except additional corn syrup and finely chopped nuts. Shape into two 10-inch logs. Brush with additional corn syrup; roll in finely chopped nuts. Wrap tightly; refrigerate 3 to 4 days to blend flavors. To serve, cut into ¹/₄-inch slices.

Makes two 10-inch logs

CHOCO-CHERRY COOKIES SUPREME

- **2/3 cup all-purpose flour**
- **1/2 cup unsweetened cocoa**
- **1 1/2 teaspoons baking powder**
- **1/2 teaspoon salt**
- **1/3 cup butter or margarine, softened**
- **1/2 cup granulated sugar**
- **1/2 cup packed light brown sugar**
- **1/3 cup milk**
- **1 large egg**
- **1 teaspoon vanilla**
- **2 cups uncooked quick-cooking or old-fashioned oats**
- **3 ounces white baking bar or white chocolate candy bar, cut into 1/4-inch pieces**
- **1/2 cup candied cherries**

Preheat oven to 375°F. Combine flour, cocoa, baking powder and salt; set aside. Beat butter and sugars in large bowl with electric mixer at medium speed until light and fluffy. Beat in milk, egg and vanilla, scraping down side of bowl once. Gradually add flour mixture. Stir in oats until well blended. Stir in baking bar pieces and cherries. Drop heaping teaspoonfuls of dough, 2 inches apart, onto greased cookie sheets. Bake 10 minutes or until set. Let stand on cookie sheets 1 minute. Remove cookies to wire racks; cool completely. *Makes about 3 dozen cookies*

"M&M'S"® CHOCOLATE CANDIES EASY PARTY COOKIES

- **1 cup butter or margarine, softened**
- **1 cup packed light brown sugar**
- **1/2 cup granulated sugar**
- **2 eggs**
- **2 teaspoons vanilla**
- **2 1/4 cups all-purpose flour**
- **1 teaspoon salt**
- **1 teaspoon baking soda**
- **1 1/2 cups "M&M's"® Plain Chocolate Candies, divided**

Preheat oven to 375°F. Beat together butter, brown sugar and granulated sugar in large bowl until light and fluffy. Blend in eggs and vanilla. Combine flour, salt and baking soda in small bowl. Add to butter mixture; mix well. Stir in 1/2 cup of the candies. Drop dough by rounded teaspoonfuls 2 inches apart onto ungreased cookie sheets. Press additional candies into each cookie. Bake 10 to 12 minutes or until golden brown. Remove to wire racks to cool completely.

Makes about 6 dozen cookies

Choco-Cherry Cookies Supreme

MERRY CHERRY MACAROONS

- 3 egg whites
- 1/4 teaspoon cream of tartar
- 1/2 cup sugar
- 1/2 teaspoon vanilla
- 1/2 teaspoon almond extract
- 1 1/3 cups (3 1/2 ounces) flaked coconut
- 1/2 cup chopped red glacé cherries
- Red glacé cherry halves (optional)

Preheat oven to 325°F. Grease cookie sheets or line (foil, waxed paper or parchment paper). In small bowl, beat egg whites and cream of tartar at high speed until foamy. Add sugar, 1 tablespoon at a time, beating constantly until sugar is dissolved* and whites are glossy and stand in soft peaks. Beat in flavorings. Stir together coconut and chopped cherries. Gently, but thoroughly, fold into beaten whites. Drop by rounded tablespoonfuls 2 inches apart onto prepared cookie sheet. Top each cookie with cherry half, if desired.

Bake 18 to 20 minutes until lightly browned. Remove to wire racks to cool completely. Store in airtight container between sheets of foil or waxed paper. *Makes 3 1/2 to 4 dozen cookies*

*Rub a bit of meringue between fingers to feel if sugar has dissolved.

Favorite recipe from American Egg Board

LEMON WAFERS

- 3/4 cup (1 1/2 sticks) margarine, softened
- 1/2 cup sugar
- 1 egg
- 1 tablespoon grated lemon peel (about 1 medium lemon)
- 2 cups QUAKER® or AUNT JEMIMA® Enriched Corn Meal
- 1 1/2 cups all-purpose flour
- 1/2 teaspoon salt (optional)
- 1/4 cup milk

Preheat oven to 375°F. Beat margarine and sugar until fluffy. Blend in egg and lemon peel. Add combined dry ingredients alternately with milk, mixing well after each addition.

Shape into 1-inch balls. Place 2 inches apart on ungreased cookie sheet. Using bottom of greased glass dipped in sugar, press into 1/8-inch-thick circles. Bake 13 to 15 minutes or until bottoms are lightly browned. Cool 2 minutes on cookie sheet; remove to wire rack. Cool completely. Store tightly covered. *Makes about 3 dozen cookies*

GOOEY CARAMEL CHOCOLATE BARS

- 2 cups all-purpose flour
- 1 cup granulated sugar
- 1/4 teaspoon salt
- 2 cups butter or margarine, divided
- 1 cup packed light brown sugar
- 1/3 cup light corn syrup
- 1 cup (6 ounces) semisweet chocolate chips

Preheat oven to 350°F. Line 13×9-inch baking pan with foil. Combine flour, granulated sugar and salt in medium bowl; stir until blended. Cut in 14 tablespoons (1 3/4 sticks) butter until mixture resembles course crumbs. Press into bottom of prepared pan.

Bake 18 to 20 minutes until lightly browned around edges. Remove pan to wire rack; cool completely.

Combine 1 cup butter, brown sugar and corn syrup in heavy medium saucepan. Cook over medium heat 5 to 8 minutes until mixture boils, stirring frequently. Boil gently 2 minutes, without stirring. Immediately pour over cooled base; spread evenly to edges of pan with metal spatula. Cool completely.

Melt chocolate in double boiler over hot (not simmering) water. Stir in remaining 2 tablespoons butter. Pour over cooled caramel layer and spread evenly to edges of pan with metal spatula. Refrigerate 10 to 15 minutes until chocolate begins to set. Remove; cool completely. Cut into bars.

Makes 3 dozen bars

DOUBLE ALMOND BUTTER COOKIES

- 2 cups butter or margarine, softened
- 2 1/2 cups powdered sugar, sifted and divided
- 4 cups all-purpose flour
- 2 1/4 teaspoons vanilla, divided
- 2/3 cup BLUE DIAMOND® Blanched Almond Paste
- 1/2 cup BLUE DIAMOND® Chopped Natural Almonds, toasted
- 1/4 cup firmly packed light brown sugar

Cream butter with 1 cup of the powdered sugar in large bowl until light and fluffy. Gradually beat in flour. Beat in 2 teaspoons of the vanilla. Cover and chill 30 minutes.

Preheat oven to 350°F. Combine almond paste, almonds, brown sugar and remaining 1/4 teaspoon vanilla. Shape dough around 1/2 teaspoon almond paste mixture; form into 1-inch balls. Place on ungreased cookie sheets.

Bake 15 minutes or until set. Remove to wire racks to cool. Roll in remaining 1 1/2 cups powdered sugar or sift the powdered sugar over cookies.

Makes about 8 dozen cookies

HOLIDAY CHOCOLATE CHIP COOKIES

- 2¼ cups all-purpose flour
- 1¼ teaspoons baking powder
- ¼ teaspoon salt
- 1 cup (2 sticks) butter, softened
- 1¼ cups sugar
- 1 egg
- 1 teaspoon vanilla extract
- One 12-ounce package (2 cups) NESTLÉ® Toll House® semi-sweet chocolate morsels
- 1 cup chopped nuts
- Three 6-ounce jars (30) maraschino cherries, drained, patted dry
- 8 small candy spearmint leaves, cut into quarters lengthwise and halved

Preheat oven to 350°F. In small bowl, combine flour, baking powder and salt; set aside.

In large mixer bowl, beat butter and sugar until creamy. Beat in egg and vanilla extract. Gradually blend in flour mixture. Stir in Nestlé® Toll House® semi-sweet chocolate morsels and nuts. Spread in greased 13×9-inch baking pan. Press 30 maraschino cherries into dough, spacing them to form six rows, five cherries per row. Place 2 spearmint "leaves" at base of each cherry; press into dough.

Bake 25 to 30 minutes. Cool completely. Cut into 2-inch squares.

Makes 30 cookies

HIDDEN TREASURES

- ⅔ BUTTER FLAVOR CRISCO® Stick or ⅔ cup BUTTER FLAVOR CRISCO all-vegetable shortening
- ¾ cup sugar
- 1 egg
- 1 tablespoon milk
- 1 teaspoon vanilla
- 1¾ cups all-purpose flour
- 1 teaspoon baking powder
- ½ teaspoon salt
- ½ teaspoon baking soda
- 48 maraschino cherries, well drained on paper towels

WHITE DIPPING CHOCOLATE

- 1 cup white melting chocolate
- 2 tablespoons BUTTER FLAVOR CRISCO® Stick or 2 tablespoons BUTTER FLAVOR CRISCO all-vegetable shortening

DARK DIPPING CHOCOLATE

- 1 cup semisweet chocolate chips
- 2 tablespoons BUTTER FLAVOR CRISCO® Stick or 2 tablespoons BUTTER FLAVOR CRISCO all-vegetable shortening

Finely chopped pecans
Slivered white chocolate

Continued

1. Preheat oven to 350°F. Cream shortening, sugar, egg, milk and vanilla in large bowl at medium speed of electric mixer until well blended.

2. Combine flour, baking powder, salt and baking soda. Beat into creamed mixture at low speed. Divide into 48 equal pieces.

3. Press dough into very thin layer around well-drained cherries. Place 2 inches apart on ungreased baking sheet.

4. Bake 10 minutes. Cool 1 minute on baking sheet. Remove to wire rack to cool completely.

5. For dipping chocolate, place chocolate of choice and shortening in glass measuring cup. Microwave at 50% (MEDIUM). Stir after 1 minute. Repeat until smooth (or melt on range top in small saucepan on very low heat).

6. Drop one cookie at a time into chocolate. Use fork to turn. Cover completely with chocolate.* Lift cookie out of chocolate with fork. Allow excess to drip off. Place on waxed paper-lined baking sheet.

7. Sprinkle chopped pecans on top of white chocolate cookies before chocolate sets. Sprinkle white chocolate on dark chocolate cookies before chocolate sets. Chill in refrigerator to set chocolate.

Makes about 4 dozen cookies

*If chocolate becomes too firm, reheat in microwave or on range top.

Hidden Treasures

Walnut Christmas Balls

WALNUT CHRISTMAS BALLS

1 cup California walnuts
2/3 cup powdered sugar, divided
1 cup butter or margarine, softened
1 teaspoon vanilla
1 3/4 cups all-purpose flour
Chocolate Filling (recipe follows)

Preheat oven to 350°F. In food processor or blender, process walnuts with 2 tablespoons of the sugar until finely ground; set aside. In large bowl, cream butter and remaining sugar. Beat in vanilla. Add flour and 3/4 cup of the ground walnuts; mix until blended. Roll dough into about 3 dozen walnut-size balls. Place 2 inches apart on ungreased cookie sheets.

Bake 10 to 12 minutes or until just golden around edges. Remove to wire racks to cool completely.

Prepare Chocolate Filling. Place generous teaspoonful of filling on flat side of half of the cookies. Top with remaining cookies, flat side down, forming sandwiches. Roll chocolate edges of cookies in remaining ground walnuts. *Makes about 1 1/2 dozen sandwich cookies*

Continued

Chocolate Filling: Chop 3 squares (1 ounce each) semisweet chocolate into small pieces; place in food processor or blender with 1/2 teaspoon vanilla. In small saucepan, heat 2 tablespoons *each* butter or margarine and whipping cream over medium heat until hot; pour over chocolate. Process until chocolate is melted, turning machine off and scraping side as needed. With machine running, gradually add 1 cup powdered sugar; process until smooth.

Favorite recipe from Walnut Marketing Board

CARAMEL PECAN COOKIES

COOKIE

- **1/2 cup BUTTER FLAVOR CRISCO® all-vegetable shortening, melted**
- **1 package DUNCAN HINES® Moist Deluxe Yellow Cake Mix**
- **1 cup JIF® Extra Crunchy Peanut Butter**
- **2 eggs**
- **2 tablespoons orange juice or water**

CARAMEL AND CHOCOLATE TOPPING

- **28 caramels**
- **2 tablespoons milk**
- **2 cups pecan halves**
- **1 package (6 ounces) semisweet chocolate chips**

1. Preheat oven to 350°F. For cookie, combine shortening, Duncan Hines® Yellow Cake Mix, Jif® Extra Crunchy Peanut Butter, eggs and juice in large bowl. Beat at medium speed of electric mixer until well blended.

2. Drop rounded tablespoonfuls of dough, 3 inches apart, onto ungreased cookie sheet.

3. Bake 10 to 12 minutes or until set. Cool 1 minute on cookie sheet. Remove to wire rack to cool completely.

4. For topping, combine caramels and milk in microwave-safe bowl. Cover with waxed paper. Microwave at 50% (MEDIUM). Stir after 1 minute. Repeat until smooth (or melt on range top in small saucepan on very low heat). Drop rounded teaspoonfuls on top of each cookie. Place 3 pecan halves around edge of caramel to resemble turtles.

5. Place chocolate chips in microwave-safe cup. Microwave at 50% (MEDIUM). Stir after 1 minute. Repeat until smooth (or melt on range top in small saucepan on very low heat). Spread rounded teaspoonfuls over top of caramel. Do not cover the pecans. Cool completely.

Makes about 4 dozen cookies

Cookie Cutter Cutouts

Decorating cutout cookies is great fun for the family. Use frostings, colored sugars, candied fruit, chopped nuts, small candies and your imagination.

SPICY GINGERBREAD COOKIES

COOKIES
- **1/2 cup firmly packed brown sugar**
- **3/4 cup (1 1/4 sticks) butter or margarine, softened**
- **2/3 cup light molasses**
- **1 egg**
- **1 1/2 teaspoons grated lemon peel**
- **2 1/2 cups all-purpose flour**
- **1 1/4 teaspoons ground cinnamon**
- **1 teaspoon vanilla**
- **1 teaspoon ground allspice**
- **1/2 teaspoon ground ginger**
- **1/2 teaspoon baking soda**
- **1/2 teaspoon salt**
- **1/4 teaspoon baking powder**

FROSTING
- **4 cups powdered sugar**
- **1/2 cup butter, softened**
- **4 tablespoons milk**
- **2 teaspoons vanilla**
- **Food coloring**

For Cookies, in large mixer bowl, combine brown sugar, butter, molasses, egg and lemon peel. Beat at medium speed, scraping bowl often, until smooth and creamy, 1 to 2 minutes. Add all remaining cookie ingredients. Reduce speed to low. Continue beating, scraping bowl often, until well mixed, 1 to 2 minutes. Cover; refrigerate at least 2 hours.

Preheat oven to 350°F. On well floured surface, roll out dough, one half at a time (keeping remaining dough refrigerated), to 1/4-inch thickness. Cut with 3- to 4-inch cookie cutters. Place, 1 inch apart, on greased cookie sheets. Bake for 6 to 8 minutes or until no indentation remains when touched. Remove immediately. Cool completely.

For Frosting, in small mixer bowl combine powdered sugar, butter, milk and vanilla. Beat at low speed, scraping bowl often, until fluffy, 1 to 2 minutes. If desired, color frosting with food coloring. Decorate cookies with frosting.

Makes about 4 dozen cookies

Spicy Gingerbread Cookies

To:
SANTA

Cream Cheese Cutout Cookies

CREAM CHEESE CUTOUT COOKIES

1 cup butter, softened
1 package (8 ounces) cream cheese, softened
$1^1/_2$ cups sugar
1 egg
1 teaspoon vanilla
$^1/_2$ teaspoon almond extract
$3^1/_2$ cups all-purpose flour
1 teaspoon baking powder
Almond Frosting (recipe follows)
Assorted candies for decoration (optional)

In large bowl, beat butter and cream cheese until well combined. Add sugar; beat until fluffy. Add egg, vanilla and almond extract; beat well. In small bowl, combine flour and baking powder. Add dry ingredients to cream cheese mixture; beat until well mixed. Divide dough in half. Wrap each portion in plastic wrap; refrigerate about $1^1/_2$ hours.

Continued

Preheat oven to 375°F. Roll out dough, half at a time, to 1/8-inch thickness on lightly floured surface. Cut out with cookie cutters. Place 2 inches apart on ungreased cookie sheets.

Bake 8 to 10 minutes or until edges are lightly browned. Remove to wire racks to cool completely. Frost cookies with Almond Frosting; decorate with assorted candies, if desired. *Makes about 7 dozen cookies*

Almond Frosting: In small bowl, beat 2 cups sifted powdered sugar, 2 tablespoons softened butter and 1/4 teaspoon almond extract until smooth. For piping consistency, beat in 4 to 5 teaspoons milk. For spreading consistency, add a little more milk. If desired, tint with food coloring.

Favorite recipe from Wisconsin Milk Marketing Board

PEANUT BUTTER GINGERBREAD MEN

- **5 cups all-purpose flour**
- **1½ teaspoons ground cinnamon**
- **1 teaspoon baking soda**
- **½ teaspoon ground ginger**
- **¼ teaspoon salt**
- **¾ cup MAZOLA® Margarine, softened**
- **¾ cup SKIPPY® Creamy Peanut Butter**
- **1 cup packed brown sugar**
- **1 cup KARO® Dark Corn Syrup**
- **2 eggs**
- **Frosting for decorating (optional)**

In large bowl, combine flour, cinnamon, baking soda, ginger and salt. In another large bowl, beat margarine and peanut butter until well blended. Add brown sugar, corn syrup and eggs; beat until smooth. Gradually beat in 2 cups of the dry ingredients. With wooden spoon, beat in remaining dry ingredients, 1 cup at a time, until well blended. Divide dough into thirds. Wrap in plastic wrap; chill until firm, at least 1 hour.

Preheat oven to 300°F. Roll out dough, one third at a time, to 1/8-inch thickness on lightly floured surface. Cut out with 5½-inch gingerbread cutter. Place 2 inches apart on ungreased cookie sheets.

Bake 10 to 12 minutes or until lightly browned. Remove to wire racks to cool completely. Pipe frosting on cookies to make eyes and buttons, if desired. *Makes about 2½ dozen cookies*

DUTCH ST. NICHOLAS COOKIES

¾ cup butter or margarine, softened
½ cup packed brown sugar
2 tablespoons milk
1½ teaspoons ground cinnamon
¼ teaspoon ground nutmeg
¼ teaspoon ground ginger
¼ teaspoon ground cloves
2 cups sifted all-purpose flour
1½ teaspoons baking powder
½ teaspoon salt
½ cup toasted chopped almonds
¼ cup coarsely chopped citron

In large bowl, cream butter, sugar, milk and spices. In small bowl, combine flour, baking powder and salt. Add flour mixture to creamed mixture; blend well. Stir in almonds and citron. Knead dough slightly to make ball. Cover; chill until firm.

Preheat oven to 375°F. Grease cookie sheets. Roll out dough to ¼-inch thickness on lightly floured surface. Cut out with cookie cutters. Place 2 inches apart on prepared cookie sheets. Bake 7 to 10 minutes or until lightly browned. Remove to wire racks to cool.

Makes about 3½ dozen cookies

Favorite recipe from Almond Board of California

FESTIVE LEBKUCHEN

3 tablespoons butter or margarine
1 cup packed brown sugar
¼ cup honey
1 egg
Grated peel and juice of 1 lemon
3 cups all-purpose flour
2 teaspoons ground allspice
½ teaspoon baking soda
½ teaspoon salt
White decorators frosting

Melt butter with brown sugar and honey in medium saucepan over low heat, stirring constantly. Pour into large bowl. Cool 30 minutes. Add egg, lemon peel and juice; beat 2 minutes with electric mixer on high speed. Stir in flour, allspice, baking soda and salt until well blended. Cover; refrigerate overnight or up to 3 days.

Preheat oven to 350°F. Grease cookie sheet. Roll out dough to ½-inch thickness on lightly floured surface with lightly floured rolling pin. Cut with 3-inch cookie cutter. Transfer to prepared cookie sheet. Bake 15 to 18 minutes until edges are light brown. Cool 1 minute. Remove to wire rack; cool completely. Decorate with white frosting. Store in airtight container.

Makes 1 dozen cookies

PEANUT BUTTER CUTOUT COOKIES

1 cup REESE'S® Peanut Butter Chips
1/2 cup butter or margarine
2/3 cup packed light brown sugar
1 egg
3/4 teaspoon vanilla extract
1 1/3 cups all-purpose flour
3/4 teaspoon baking soda
1/2 cup finely chopped pecans
Chocolate Chip Glaze (recipe follows)

Melt peanut butter chips and butter in medium saucepan over low heat, stirring constantly. Pour into large mixer bowl; add brown sugar, egg and vanilla, beating until well blended. Stir in flour, baking soda and pecans; blend well. Cover and chill 15 to 20 minutes or until firm enough to roll.

Preheat oven to 350°F. Roll out dough, a small portion at a time, to 1/4-inch thickness on lightly floured surface. (Keep remaining dough in refrigerator.) With cookie cutters, cut into desired shapes. Place 2 inches apart on ungreased cookie sheets.

Bake 7 to 8 minutes or until almost set (do not overbake). Cool 1 minute. Remove to wire racks to cool completely. Drizzle Chocolate Chip Glaze onto each cookie; allow to set. *Makes about 3 dozen cookies*

Chocolate Chip Glaze: Melt 1 cup HERSHEY'S Semi-Sweet Chocolate Chips with 1 tablespoon shortening in top of double boiler over hot, not boiling, water; stir until smooth. Remove from heat; cool slightly, stirring occasionally.

Peanut Butter Cutout Cookies

PHILLY CREAM CHEESE COOKIE DOUGH

1 (8-ounce) package PHILADELPHIA BRAND® Cream Cheese, softened
3/4 cup butter, softened
1 cup powdered sugar
2 1/4 cups all-purpose flour
1/2 teaspoon baking soda

Beat cream cheese, butter and sugar in large mixing bowl at medium speed with electric mixer until well blended.

Add flour and soda; mix well. *Makes 3 cups dough*

CHOCOLATE MINT CUTOUTS

Preheat oven to 325°F.

Add 1/4 teaspoon mint extract and few drops green food coloring to 1 1/2 cups Cookie Dough; mix well. Chill 30 minutes.

On lightly floured surface, roll dough to 1/8-inch thickness; cut with assorted 3-inch cookie cutters. Place on ungreased cookie sheet.

Bake 10 to 12 minutes or until edges begin to brown. Cool on wire rack.

Melt 1/4 cup mint flavored semi-sweet chocolate chips in small saucepan over low heat, stirring until smooth. Drizzle over cookies.

Makes about 3 dozen cookies

SNOWMEN

Preheat oven to 325°F.

Add 1/4 teaspoon vanilla to 1 1/2 cups Cookie Dough; mix well. Chill 30 minutes.

For each snowman, shape dough into two small balls, one slightly larger than the other. Place balls, slightly overlapping, on ungreased cookie sheet; flatten with bottom of glass. Repeat with remaining dough.

Bake 18 to 20 minutes or until light golden brown. Cool on wire rack.

Sprinkle each snowman with sifted powdered sugar. Decorate with icing as desired. Cut miniature peanut butter cups in half for hats.

Makes about 2 dozen cookies

Continued

Clockwise from top left: Preserve Thumbprints (page 32); Snowmen; Choco-Orange Slices (page 32); Chocolate Mint Cutouts

CHOCO-ORANGE SLICES

Preheat oven to 325°F.

Add 1½ teaspoons grated orange peel to 1½ cups Cookie Dough; mix well. Shape into 8×1½-inch log. Chill 30 minutes.

Cut log into ¼-inch slices. Place on ungreased cookie sheet.

Bake 15 to 18 minutes or until edges begin to brown. Cool on wire rack.

Melt ⅓ cup BAKER'S® Semi-Sweet Real Chocolate Chips with 1 tablespoon orange juice and 1 tablespoon orange flavored liqueur in small saucepan over low heat, stirring until smooth. Dip cookies into chocolate mixture. *Makes about 2½ dozen cookies*

PRESERVE THUMBPRINTS

Preheat oven to 325°F.

Add ½ cup chopped pecans and ½ teaspoon vanilla to 1½ cups Cookie Dough; mix well. Chill 30 minutes.

Shape dough into 1-inch balls. Place on ungreased cookie sheet. Indent centers; fill each with 1 teaspoon KRAFT® Preserves.

Bake 14 to 16 minutes or until light golden brown. Cool on wire rack.
Makes about 3⅓ dozen cookies

CHOCOLATE CANDY THUMBPRINTS

Preheat oven to 325°F.

Add ½ cup chopped pecans and ½ teaspoon vanilla to 1½ cups Cookie Dough; mix well. Chill 30 minutes.

Shape dough into 1-inch balls. Place on ungreased cookie sheet. Indent centers.

Bake 14 to 16 minutes or until light golden brown.

Immediately place milk chocolate candy kiss in center of each cookie. Let stand 1 to 2 minutes or until chocolate is slightly softened; spread over top of cookies. Cool on wire rack. *Makes about 3½ dozen cookies*

COCOA GINGERBREAD COOKIES

- 1/4 cup butter or margarine, softened
- 2 tablespoons shortening
- 1/3 cup packed brown sugar
- 1/4 cup dark molasses
- 1 egg
- 1 1/2 cups all-purpose flour
- 1/4 cup unsweetened cocoa
- 1/2 teaspoon baking soda
- 1/2 teaspoon ground ginger
- 1/2 teaspoon ground cinnamon
- 1/4 teaspoon salt
- 1/4 teaspoon ground nutmeg
- 1/8 teaspoon ground cloves
- Decorator Icing (recipe follows)

Preheat oven to 400°F. Lightly grease cookie sheets or line with parchment paper. Cream butter, shortening, brown sugar and molasses in large bowl. Add egg; beat until light. Combine flour, cocoa, baking soda, ginger, cinnamon, salt, nutmeg and cloves in small bowl. Blend into creamed mixture until smooth. (If dough is too soft to handle, cover and refrigerate until firm.)

Roll out dough to 1/4-inch thickness on lightly floured surface. Cut out with cookie cutters. Place 2 inches apart on prepared cookie sheets.

Bake 8 to 10 minutes or until firm. Remove to wire racks to cool completely.

Prepare Decorator Icing. Spoon into pastry bag fitted with small tip. Decorate cookies with icing. *Makes about 6 dozen cookies*

Decorator Icing: Combine 4 cups powdered sugar and 2 tablespoons milk in large bowl; mix until smooth. Add 1 teaspoon almond or lemon extract; mix well. Add more milk as necessary until smooth and glossy.

Lemon Cut-Out Cookies

LEMON CUT-OUT COOKIES

- **2¾ cups unsifted all-purpose flour**
- **1 teaspoon baking powder**
- **½ teaspoon baking soda**
- **¼ teaspoon salt**
- **1½ cups sugar**
- **½ cup margarine or butter, softened**
- **1 egg**
- **⅓ cup REALEMON® Lemon Juice from Concentrate**
- **Lemon Icing (recipe follows) (optional)**

Sift together flour, baking powder, baking soda and salt; set aside. In large mixer bowl, beat sugar and margarine until fluffy; beat in egg. Gradually add dry ingredients alternately with ReaLemon® brand; mix well (dough will be soft). Cover and chill overnight in refrigerator or 2 hours in freezer.

Continued

Preheat oven to 375°F. Grease cookie sheets. On well-floured surface, roll out dough, one third at a time, to 1/8-inch thickness; cut with floured cookie cutters. Place 1 inch apart on prepared cookie sheets.

Bake 8 to 10 minutes. Remove to wire racks to cool completely. Repeat with remaining dough. Ice and decorate as desired.

Makes 4 to 5 dozen cookies

Lemon Icing: Mix 1 1/4 cups confectioners' sugar and 2 tablespoons ReaLemon® brand until smooth. Add food coloring, if desired.

Makes about 1/2 cup

CONFETTI CUTOUTS

COOKIES
1 1/2 cups sugar
2/3 cup butter or margarine, softened
2 eggs
1 tablespoon milk
1 1/2 teaspoons almond extract
3 1/2 cups all-purpose flour
2 1/2 teaspoons baking powder
1/2 teaspoon salt

FILLING
1/4 cup vegetable shortening
1 1/2 cups "M&M'S"® Plain Chocolate Candies

For cookies, in large bowl beat together sugar and butter until light and fluffy; blend in eggs, milk and extract. In bowl combine flour, baking powder and salt. Gradually add dry ingredients, mixing well after each addition. Cover and chill dough several hours.

Preheat oven to 400°F. Roll out dough, one fourth at a time, to 1/8-inch thickness on floured surface. Cut with floured 2 1/2-inch cookie cutters. Cut out small designs in centers of half the cookies with smaller cutter or sharp knife. Place 2 inches apart on ungreased cookie sheets.

Bake 7 to 9 minutes or until edges are very light golden brown. Remove to wire racks to cool completely.

For filling, melt shortening in 2-quart heavy saucepan; add candies. Cook over very low heat, stirring constantly with metal spoon and pressing candies with back of spoon to break up. (Chocolate will be almost melted and pieces of color coating will remain.) Cool slightly or until of spreading consistency. Spread solid cookies with warm filling; top with cutout cookies, pressing lightly to secure. Chill about 30 minutes to set chocolate. Store at room temperature. *Makes about 3 dozen cookies*

CUT-OUT SUGAR COOKIES

2/3 BUTTER FLAVOR CRISCO® Stick or 2/3 cup BUTTER FLAVOR CRISCO all-vegetable shortening
3/4 cup sugar
1 tablespoon plus 1 teaspoon milk
1 teaspoon vanilla
1 egg
2 cups all-purpose flour
1 1/2 teaspoons baking powder
1/4 teaspoon salt
Colored sugars and decors for garnish

1. Cream shortening, sugar, milk and vanilla in large bowl at medium speed of electric mixer until well blended. Beat in egg.

2. Combine flour, baking powder and salt. Mix into creamed mixture at low speed until well blended. Cover and refrigerate several hours or overnight.

3. Preheat oven to 375°F. Roll out dough, half at a time, on floured surface to 1/8-inch thickness. Cut into desired shapes. Place 2 inches apart on ungreased baking sheet. Sprinkle with colored sugars and decors or leave plain to frost when cool.

4. Bake 7 to 9 minutes or until set. Remove immediately to wire racks to cool completely.

Makes about 3 dozen cookies (depending on size and shape)

Variations

Creamy Vanilla Frosting: Combine 1/2 cup Butter Flavor Crisco®, 1 pound (4 cups) powdered sugar, 1/3 cup milk and 1 teaspoon vanilla in medium bowl. Beat at low speed of electric mixer until well blended. Scrape bowl. Beat at high speed for 2 minutes, or until smooth and creamy. One or two drops food color can be used to tint each cup of frosting, if desired. Frost cooled cookies. This frosting works well in decorating tube.

Chocolate Dipped Sugar Cookies: Bake and cool cookies. Combine 1 cup semi-sweet chocolate chips and 1 teaspoon Butter Flavor Crisco® in microwave-safe measuring cup. Microwave at 50% power (MEDIUM). Stir after 1 minute. Repeat until smooth (or melt on range top in small saucepan on very low heat). Dip one end of cooled cookie halfway up in chocolate. Place on waxed paper until chocolate is firm.

Chocolate Nut Sugar Cookies: Dip in melted chocolate as directed for Chocolate Dipped Sugar Cookies. Spread with finely chopped nuts before chocolate hardens.

Cut-Out Sugar Cookies

Lemony Butter Cookies

LEMONY BUTTER COOKIES

- ½ cup butter, softened
- ½ cup sugar
- 1 egg
- 1½ cups all-purpose flour
- 2 tablespoons fresh lemon juice
- 1 teaspoon grated lemon peel
- ½ teaspoon baking powder
- ⅛ teaspoon salt
- Additional sugar

Continued

Beat butter and sugar in large bowl with electric mixer until creamy. Beat in egg until light and fluffy. Mix in flour, lemon juice and peel, baking powder and salt. Cover; refrigerate about 2 hours or until firm.

Preheat oven to 350°F. Roll out dough, a small portion at a time, to 1/4-inch thickness on well-floured surface with floured rolling pin. (Keep remaining dough in refrigerator.) Cut with 3-inch round cookie cutter. Transfer to ungreased cookie sheets. Sprinkle with sugar.

Bake 8 to 10 minutes until lightly browned on edges. Cool 1 minute on cookie sheets. Remove to wire racks; cool completely. Store in airtight container. *Makes about 2 1/2 dozen cookies*

CHOCOLATE KAHLÚA® BEARS

- **1/4 cup KAHLÚA®**
- **2 squares (1 ounce each) unsweetened chocolate**
- **1 2/3 cups sugar**
- **2/3 cup shortening**
- **2 eggs**
- **2 teaspoons vanilla**
- **2 cups sifted all-purpose flour**
- **2 teaspoons baking powder**
- **3/4 teaspoon salt**
- **1/2 teaspoon ground cinnamon**
- **Chocolate Icing (recipe follows)**

To Kahlúa® in measuring cup, add enough water to make 1/3 cup liquid. In small saucepan over low heat, melt chocolate; cool. In large bowl, beat sugar, shortening, eggs and vanilla until light and fluffy. Stir in chocolate. In small bowl, combine flour, baking powder, salt and cinnamon. Add dry ingredients to egg mixture alternately with 1/3 cup liquid. Cover; chill until firm.

Preheat oven to 350°F. Roll out dough, one fourth at a time, to 1/4-inch thickness on well-floured surface. Cut out with bear-shaped cookie cutters. Place 2 inches apart on ungreased cookie sheets.

Bake 8 to 10 minutes. Remove to wire racks to cool completely. Spread Chocolate Icing in thin, even layer on cookies. Let stand until set; decorate as desired. *Makes about 2 1/2 dozen cookies*

Chocolate Icing: In medium saucepan, combine 6 squares (1 ounce each) semisweet chocolate, 1/3 cup butter or margarine, 1/4 cup Kahlúa® and 1 tablespoon light corn syrup. Cook over low heat until chocolate melts, stirring to blend. Add 3/4 cup sifted powdered sugar; beat until smooth. If necessary, beat in additional Kahlúa® to make spreading consistency.

Heavenly Chocolate

Chocolate lovers look no further. All the cookies in this chapter are chocolatey-good—some are even drizzled with or dipped into luscious chocolate!

CHOCOLATE CHERRY COOKIES

2 squares (1 ounce each) unsweetened chocolate
½ cup butter or margarine, softened
½ cup sugar
1 egg
2 cups cake flour
1 teaspoon vanilla
¼ teaspoon salt
Maraschino cherries, well drained (about 48)
1 cup (6 ounces) semisweet or milk chocolate chips

Melt unsweetened chocolate in top of double boiler over hot, not boiling, water. Remove from heat; cool. Cream butter and sugar in large bowl until light. Add egg and melted chocolate; beat until fluffy. Stir in flour, vanilla and salt until well blended. Cover; refrigerate until firm, about 1 hour.

Preheat oven to 400°F. Lightly grease cookie sheets or line with parchment paper. Shape dough into 1-inch balls. Place 2 inches apart on prepared cookie sheets. With knuckle of finger, make a deep indentation in center of each ball. Place a cherry into each indentation.

Bake 8 minutes or just until set. Meanwhile, melt chocolate chips in small bowl over hot water. Stir until melted. Remove cookies to wire racks to cool. Drizzle melted chocolate over tops while still warm. Refrigerate until chocolate is set. *Makes about 4 dozen cookies*

Top: Chocolate Spritz (page 43) and Chocolate Cherry Cookies
Bottom: Triple Chocolate Pretzels (page 42)

TRIPLE CHOCOLATE PRETZELS

Buttery pretzel-shaped chocolate cookies are glazed with dark chocolate, then decorated with white chocolate for a triple chocolate treat.

2 squares (1 ounce each) unsweetened chocolate
½ cup butter or margarine, softened
½ cup granulated sugar
1 egg
2 cups cake flour
1 teaspoon vanilla
¼ teaspoon salt
Mocha Glaze (recipe follows)
2 ounces white chocolate, chopped

Melt unsweetened chocolate in top of double boiler over hot, not boiling, water. Remove from heat; cool. Cream butter and granulated sugar in large bowl until light and fluffy. Add egg and melted chocolate; beat until fluffy. Stir in cake flour, vanilla and salt until well blended. Cover; chill until firm, about 1 hour.

Preheat oven to 400°F. Lightly grease cookie sheets or line with parchment paper. Divide dough into 4 equal parts. Divide each part into 12 pieces. To form pretzels, knead each piece briefly to soften dough. Roll into a rope about 6 inches long. Form each rope on prepared cookie sheet into a pretzel shape. Repeat with all pieces of dough, spacing cookies 2 inches apart.

Bake 7 to 9 minutes or until firm. Remove to wire racks to cool. Prepare Mocha Glaze. Dip pretzels, one at a time, into glaze to coat completely. Place on waxed paper, right side up. Let stand until glaze is set. Melt white chocolate in small bowl over hot water. Squeeze melted chocolate through pastry bag or drizzle over pretzels to decorate. Let stand until chocolate is completely set. *Makes 4 dozen cookies*

MOCHA GLAZE

1 cup (6 ounces) semisweet chocolate chips
1 teaspoon light corn syrup
1 teaspoon shortening
1 cup powdered sugar
3 to 5 tablespoons hot coffee or water

Combine chocolate chips, corn syrup and shortening in small heavy saucepan. Stir over low heat until chocolate is melted. Stir in powdered sugar and enough coffee to make a smooth glaze.

CHOCOLATE SPRITZ

2 squares (1 ounce each) unsweetened chocolate
1 cup butter, softened
½ cup granulated sugar
1 egg
1 teaspoon vanilla
¼ teaspoon salt
2¼ cups all-purpose flour
Powdered sugar

Preheat oven to 400°F. Line cookie sheets with parchment paper or leave ungreased. Melt chocolate in top of double boiler over hot, not boiling, water. Remove from heat; cool. Cream butter, granulated sugar, egg, vanilla and salt in large bowl until light and fluffy. Blend in melted chocolate and flour until stiff. Fit cookie press with your choice of plate. Load press with dough. Press cookies out 2 inches apart onto prepared cookie sheets.

Bake 5 to 7 minutes or just until very slightly browned around edges. Remove to wire rack to cool. Dust with powdered sugar.

Makes about 5 dozen cookies

CHOCOLATE COOKIE SANDWICHES

½ cup shortening
1 cup sugar
1 egg
1 teaspoon vanilla extract
1½ cups all-purpose flour
⅓ cup HERSHEY®'S Cocoa
½ teaspoon baking soda
½ teaspoon salt
¼ cup milk
Creme Filling (recipe follows)

Preheat oven to 375°F. In large bowl, cream shortening, sugar, egg and vanilla until light and fluffy. Combine flour, cocoa, baking soda and salt; add alternately with milk to creamed mixture until ingredients are combined. Drop by teaspoonfuls onto ungreased cookie sheets.

Bake 11 to 12 minutes or just until soft-set *(do not overbake)*. Cool 1 minute. Remove from cookie sheets; cool completely on wire rack. Prepare Creme Filling. Spread bottom of one cookie with about 1 tablespoon filling; cover with another cookie. Repeat with remaining cookies and filling.

Makes about 2 dozen sandwich cookies

Creme Filling: In small bowl, cream 2 tablespoons softened butter or margarine and 2 tablespoons shortening; gradually beat in ½ cup marshmallow creme. Blend in ¾ teaspoon vanilla extract and ⅔ cup powdered sugar; beat to spreading consistency.

Nutty Clusters

NUTTY CLUSTERS

- 2 squares (1 ounce each) unsweetened chocolate
- ½ cup butter or margarine, softened
- 1 cup granulated sugar
- 1 egg
- ⅓ cup buttermilk
- 1 teaspoon vanilla
- 1¾ cups all-purpose flour
- ½ teaspoon baking soda
- 1 cup mixed salted nuts, coarsely chopped
- Chocolate Icing (recipe follows)

Preheat oven to 400°F. Line cookie sheets with parchment paper or leave ungreased. Melt chocolate in top of double boiler over hot, not boiling, water. Remove from heat; cool. Cream butter and granulated sugar in large bowl until smooth. Beat in egg, melted chocolate, buttermilk and vanilla until light. Stir in flour, baking soda and nuts. Drop dough by teaspoonfuls 2 inches apart onto cookie sheets. Bake 8 to 10 minutes or

Continued

until almost no imprint remains when touched. Immediately remove cookies from cookie sheet to wire rack. While cookies bake, prepare Chocolate Icing. Frost cookies while still warm.

Makes about 4 dozen cookies

CHOCOLATE ICING

2 squares (1 ounce each) unsweetened chocolate
2 tablespoons butter or margarine
2 cups powdered sugar
2 to 3 tablespoons water

Melt chocolate and butter in small heavy saucepan over low heat, stirring until completely melted. Add powdered sugar and water, mixing until smooth.

BURIED CHERRY COOKIES

Chocolate Frosting (recipe follows)
½ cup butter or margarine, softened
1 cup sugar
1 egg
1½ teaspoons vanilla extract
1½ cups all-purpose flour
⅓ cup HERSHEY®S Cocoa
¼ teaspoon baking powder
¼ teaspoon baking soda
¼ teaspoon salt
1 jar (10 ounces) small maraschino cherries (about 44)

Prepare Chocolate Frosting; set aside. Preheat oven to 350°F. In large bowl, cream butter, sugar, egg and vanilla until light and fluffy. Combine flour, cocoa, baking powder, baking soda and salt; gradually add to creamed mixture until well blended.

Shape dough into 1-inch balls. Place about 2 inches apart on ungreased cookie sheet. Press thumb gently in center of each cookie. Drain cherries; place one cherry in center of each cookie.

Bake 10 minutes or until edges are set; remove from cookie sheet to wire rack. Spoon scant teaspoonful frosting over cherry, spreading to cover cherry.

Makes about 3½ dozen cookies

Chocolate Frosting: In small saucepan, combine ⅔ cup sweetened condensed milk and ½ cup HERSHEY®S Semi-Sweet Chocolate Chips. Stir constantly over low heat until chips are melted and mixture is smooth, about 5 minutes. Remove from heat; cool thoroughly.

HONEY-GINGER BOURBON BALLS

1 cup gingersnap cookie crumbs
1¼ cups powdered sugar, divided
1 cup finely chopped pecans or walnuts
1 square (1 ounce) unsweetened chocolate, chopped
1½ tablespoons honey
¼ cup bourbon

Combine crumbs, 1 cup of the sugar and nuts in large bowl. Combine chocolate and honey in small bowl over hot water; stir until chocolate is melted. Blend in bourbon. Stir bourbon mixture into crumb mixture until well blended. Shape into 1-inch balls. Sprinkle remaining powdered sugar over balls. Refrigerate until firm. *Makes about 4 dozen balls*

Note: These improve with aging; store in airtight container in refrigerator. They will keep several weeks, but are best after 2 to 3 days.

CHOCOLATE TASSIES

Tassies are old-fashioned cookies that resemble miniature pecan tarts. Here, the pecan filling is enriched with chocolate.

PASTRY
2 cups all-purpose flour
1 cup butter or margarine, cold, cut into chunks
2 packages (3 ounces each) cream cheese, cold, cut into chunks

FILLING
2 tablespoons butter or margarine
2 squares (1 ounce each) unsweetened chocolate
1½ cups packed brown sugar
2 teaspoons vanilla
2 eggs, beaten
Dash salt
1½ cups chopped pecans

For pastry, place flour in large bowl. Cut in butter and cream cheese. Continue to mix until dough can be shaped into a ball. Wrap dough in plastic wrap; refrigerate 1 hour. Shape dough into 1-inch balls. Press each ball into ungreased miniature (1¾-inch) muffin pan cup, covering bottom and side of cup with dough.

Preheat oven to 350°F. For filling, melt butter and chocolate in medium-sized heavy saucepan over low heat. Remove from heat. Blend in sugar, vanilla, eggs and salt; beat until thick. Stir in pecans. Spoon about 1 teaspoon filling into each unbaked pastry shell. Bake 20 to 25 minutes or until lightly browned and filling is set. Cool in pans on wire racks. Remove from pans; store in airtight containers.

Makes about 5 dozen cookies

DOUBLE CHOCOLATE TREASURES

1 package (12 ounces) semi-sweet chocolate pieces (2 cups), divided
3/4 cup granulated sugar
1/2 cup margarine, softened
2 eggs
1 teaspoon vanilla
2 cups QUAKER® Oats (Quick or Old Fashioned, uncooked)
1 1/2 cups all-purpose flour
2 teaspoons baking powder
1/4 teaspoon salt (optional)
1/2 cup powdered sugar

Preheat oven to 350°F. In saucepan over low heat, melt 1 cup chocolate pieces, stirring constantly until smooth; cool slightly.* Beat sugar and margarine until light and fluffy. Blend in eggs, vanilla and melted chocolate. Combine oats, flour, baking powder and salt. Stir into chocolate mixture; mix well. Stir in remaining 1 cup chocolate pieces. Shape into 1-inch balls. Roll in powdered sugar, coating heavily. Place on ungreased cookie sheet.

Bake 10 to 12 minutes. Cool 2 minutes on cookie sheet; remove to wire rack. Cool completely. Store tightly covered.

Makes about 5 dozen cookies

*Microwave Directions: Place chocolate pieces in microwaveable bowl. Microwave at HIGH 1 to 1 1/2 minutes, stirring after 1 minute. Stir until smooth.

DOUBLE CHOCOLATE BLACK-EYED SUSANS

1 package (18.25 or 19.75 ounces) fudge marble cake mix
1 egg
1/3 cup vegetable oil
4 tablespoons water, divided
1 cup HERSHEY®S MINI CHIPS Semi-Sweet Chocolate

Preheat oven to 350°F. Lightly grease cookie sheets. In bowl, combine cake mix, egg, oil and 3 tablespoons water; mix with spoon until thoroughly blended. Stir in small chocolate chips. In separate bowl, combine 2/3 cup batter, chocolate packet from cake mix and remaining 1 tablespoon water; mix well.

Drop vanilla batter by rounded teaspoonfuls onto prepared cookie sheet; gently press down centers with thumb or back of spoon. Drop chocolate batter by rounded half teaspoonfuls onto top of each cookie.

Bake 10 to 12 minutes or until very lightly browned. Cool 1 minute. Remove to wire racks to cool completely.

Makes about 3 dozen cookies

CHOCOLATE MADELEINES

1¼ cups all-purpose flour
1 cup sugar
⅛ teaspoon salt
¾ cup butter, melted
⅓ cup HERSHEY®S Cocoa
3 eggs
2 egg yolks
½ teaspoon vanilla extract
Chocolate Frosting (recipe follows)

Preheat oven to 350°F. Lightly grease indentations of madeleine mold pan (each shell is 3×2 inches). In medium saucepan, stir together flour, sugar and salt. Combine melted butter and cocoa; stir into dry ingredients. In small bowl, lightly beat eggs, egg yolks and vanilla with fork until well blended; stir into chocolate mixture, blending well. Cook over very low heat, stirring constantly, until mixture is warm; *do not simmer or boil.* Remove from heat. Fill each mold half full with batter (do not overfill).

Bake 8 to 10 minutes or until wooden pick inserted in center comes out clean. Invert onto wire rack; cool completely. Prepare Chocolate Frosting; frost flat sides of cookies. Press frosted sides together, forming shells.

Makes about 1½ dozen filled cookies

Chocolate Frosting: In small bowl, stir together 1¼ cups powdered sugar and 2 tablespoons HERSHEY®S Cocoa. In small bowl, beat 2 tablespoons softened butter and ¼ cup of the cocoa mixture until light and fluffy. Gradually add remaining cocoa mixture and 2 to 2½ tablespoons milk, beating to spreading consistency. Stir in ½ teaspoon vanilla extract.

TRIPLE CHOCOLATE COOKIES

1 package DUNCAN HINES® Moist Deluxe Swiss Chocolate Cake Mix
½ cup butter or margarine, melted
1 egg
½ cup semisweet chocolate chips
½ cup milk chocolate chips
½ cup coarsely chopped white chocolate
½ cup chopped pecans

1. Preheat oven to 375°F. Combine cake mix, melted butter and egg in large bowl. Stir in all 3 chocolates and pecans.

2. Drop by rounded tablespoonfuls 2 inches apart onto ungreased cookie sheets. Bake 9 to 11 minutes. Cool 1 minute on cookie sheet. Remove to wire racks to cool completely.

Makes 3½ to 4 dozen cookies

Chocolate Madeleines

Chocolate Nut Slices

CHOCOLATE NUT SLICES

- 3/4 BUTTER FLAVOR CRISCO® Stick or 3/4 cup BUTTER FLAVOR CRISCO all-vegetable shortening
- 1/2 cup granulated sugar
- 1/3 cup firmly packed brown sugar
- 2 tablespoons milk
- 1 1/2 teaspoons vanilla
- 1 egg
- 1 1/4 cups all-purpose flour
- 1/3 cup unsweetened cocoa powder
- 1/2 teaspoon baking soda
- 1/2 teaspoon salt
- 3/4 cup coarsely chopped pecans
- 1/2 cup semisweet chocolate chips

DRIZZLE

- 1/2 teaspoon BUTTER FLAVOR CRISCO® Stick or 1/2 teaspoon BUTTER FLAVOR CRISCO all-vegetable shortening
- 1/2 cup white melting chocolate, cut into small pieces
- Chopped Pecans (optional)

Continued

1. Preheat oven to 350°F. For cookie, combine shortening, granulated sugar, brown sugar, milk and vanilla in large bowl. Beat at medium speed of electric mixer until well blended. Beat in egg.

2. Combine flour, cocoa, baking soda and salt. Mix into creamed mixture at low speed until blended. Stir in nuts and chocolate chips.

3. Divide dough into 4 equal portions. Form each into 1×8-inch roll on waxed paper. Pick up ends of waxed paper and roll dough back and forth to get a nicely shaped roll. Place 3 inches apart on ungreased baking sheet.

4. Bake 10 minutes or until set. Cool on baking sheets.

5. For drizzle, combine shortening and white chocolate in microwave-safe cup. Microwave at 50% (MEDIUM). Stir after 1 minute. Repeat until smooth (or melt on range top in small saucepan on very low heat). Drizzle back and forth over cooled cookie. Sprinkle with nuts before chocolate hardens, if desired.

6. Cut diagonally into 1-inch slices. *Makes about 3 dozen cookies*

DOUBLE CHOCOLATE CHUNK COOKIES

2 squares (1 ounce each) unsweetened chocolate
3 eggs
1 cup vegetable oil
3/4 cup packed brown sugar
1 teaspoon baking powder
1 teaspoon vanilla
1/4 teaspoon baking soda
1/4 teaspoon salt
2 1/3 cups all-purpose flour
1 package (12 ounces) semisweet chocolate chunks

Preheat oven to 350°F. Lightly grease cookie sheets or line with parchment paper. Melt unsweetened chocolate in top of double boiler over hot, not boiling, water. Remove from heat; cool. Beat eggs in large bowl until foamy. Add the oil and sugar; continue beating until light and frothy. Blend in baking powder, vanilla, baking soda, salt and melted chocolate. Mix in flour until smooth. Stir in chocolate chunks. Shape dough into walnut-sized balls. Place 2 inches apart on prepared cookie sheets. Bake 10 to 12 minutes or until firm in center. Do not overbake. Remove to wire racks to cool. *Makes about 4 1/2 dozen cookies*

White Chocolate Chunk Cookies: Substitute one package (12 ounces) white chocolate chunks *or* two white chocolate candy bars (5 to 6 ounces each), cut into chunks, for the semisweet chocolate chunks.

Bevy of Bars

Easy-to-make bars are always a favorite. Choose from buttery shortbreads, fruit-topped bars, spice bars and fudgy brownies.

PECAN DATE BARS

CRUST

1 package DUNCAN HINES® Moist Deluxe White Cake Mix
1/3 cup cold butter or margarine
1 egg

TOPPING

1 package (8 ounces) chopped dates
1 1/4 cups chopped pecans
1 cup water
1/2 teaspoon vanilla extract
Confectioners' sugar

1. Preheat oven to 350°F. Grease and flour 13×9-inch pan.

2. For crust, cut butter into cake mix with a pastry blender or 2 knives until mixture is crumbly. Add egg; stir well (mixture will be crumbly). Pat mixture into bottom of pan.

3. For topping, combine dates, pecans and water in medium saucepan. Bring to a boil. Reduce heat and simmer until mixture thickens, stirring constantly. Remove from heat. Stir in vanilla extract. Spread date mixture evenly over crust. Bake 25 to 30 minutes. Cool completely in pan on wire rack. Dust with confectioners' sugar. *Makes 32 bars*

Tip: Pecan Date Bars are moist and store well in airtight containers. Dust with confectioners' sugar to freshen before serving.

Pecan Date Bars

Almond Toffee Triangles

ALMOND TOFFEE TRIANGLES

Bar Cookie Crust (see page 70)
1/3 cup packed brown sugar
1/3 cup KARO® Light or Dark Corn Syrup
1/4 cup MAZOLA® Margarine
1/4 cup heavy cream
1 1/2 cups sliced almonds
1 teaspoon vanilla

Preheat oven to 350°F. Prepare Bar Cookie Crust. In medium saucepan combine brown sugar, corn syrup, margarine and cream. Bring to boil over medium heat; remove from heat. Stir in almonds and vanilla. Pour over hot crust; spread evenly.

Bake 15 to 20 minutes or until set and golden. Cool completely on wire rack. Cut into 2 1/2-inch squares; cut each in half diagonally to create triangles. *Makes 4 dozen triangles*

DELUXE TOLL HOUSE® MUD BARS

1 cup plus 2 tablespoons all-purpose flour
½ teaspoon baking soda
½ teaspoon salt
¾ cup firmly packed brown sugar
½ cup (1 stick) butter, softened
1 teaspoon vanilla extract
1 egg
One 12-ounce package (2 cups) NESTLÉ® Toll House® semi-sweet chocolate morsels, divided
½ cup chopped walnuts

Preheat oven to 375°F. Grease 9-inch square baking pan. In small bowl, combine flour, baking soda and salt; set aside. In large mixer bowl, beat brown sugar, butter and vanilla extract until creamy. Beat in egg. Gradually add flour mixture. Stir in 1⅓ cups Nestlé® Toll House® semi-sweet chocolate morsels and walnuts. Spread into prepared pan. Bake 23 to 25 minutes.

Immediately sprinkle remaining ⅔ cup Nestlé® Toll House® semi-sweet chocolate morsels over top. Let stand until morsels become shiny and soft. Spread chocolate with spatula. When cool, chill 5 to 10 minutes to set chocolate. Cut into 2×1½-inch square bars. *Makes 2 dozen bars*

PECAN CARAMEL BARS

1½ cups all-purpose flour
1½ cups packed brown sugar, divided
½ cup butter, softened
1 cup pecan halves
⅔ cup butter
1 cup milk chocolate pieces

Preheat oven to 350°F. In large mixer bowl, combine flour, 1 cup brown sugar and ½ cup butter. Beat 2 to 3 minutes or until mixture resembles fine crumbs. Pat mixture evenly onto bottom of ungreased 13×9-inch baking pan. Sprinkle nuts evenly over crumb mixture.

In small saucepan, combine ⅔ cup butter and remaining ½ cup brown sugar. Cook and stir over medium heat until entire surface is bubbly. Cook and stir up to 1 minute more. Pour over crust, spreading evenly.

Bake 18 to 20 minutes or until entire surface is bubbly. Remove from oven; immediately sprinkle with chocolate pieces. Let stand 2 to 3 minutes to allow chocolate to melt; use knife to swirl chocolate slightly. Cool completely on wire rack. Cut into bars. *Makes 4 dozen bars*

Favorite recipe from Wisconsin Milk Marketing Board

QUICK AND EASY NUTTY CHEESE BARS

BASE
- **1 package DUNCAN HINES® Moist Deluxe Butter Recipe Golden Cake Mix**
- **3/4 cup chopped pecans or walnuts**
- **3/4 cup butter or margarine, melted**

TOPPING
- **2 packages (8 ounces each) cream cheese, softened**
- **1 cup firmly packed brown sugar**
- **3/4 cup chopped pecans or walnuts**

1. Preheat oven to 350°F. Grease and flour 13×9-inch pan. For base, combine cake mix, 3/4 cup pecans and melted butter in large bowl. Stir until well blended. Press mixture into bottom of pan.

2. For topping, combine cream cheese and sugar in medium bowl. Stir with spoon until well mixed. Spread evenly over base. Sprinkle with 3/4 cup pecans.

3. Bake 25 to 30 minutes or until edges are browned and cheese topping is set. Cool completely in pan on wire rack. Cut into 2 1/4×2-inch bars. Refrigerate leftovers.

Makes 2 dozen bars

ENGLISH TOFFEE BARS

- **2 cups all-purpose flour**
- **1 cup packed light brown sugar**
- **1/2 cup butter**
- **1 cup pecan halves**
- **Toffee Topping (recipe follows)**
- **1 cup HERSHEY®S Milk Chocolate Chips**

Preheat oven to 350°F. In large mixer bowl, combine flour, brown sugar and butter; mix until fine crumbs form. (A few large crumbs may remain.) Press into ungreased 13×9-inch baking pan. Sprinkle pecans over crust. Prepare Toffee Topping and immediately drizzle over pecans and crust.

Bake 20 to 22 minutes or until topping is bubbly and golden. Remove from oven. Immediately sprinkle milk chocolate chips over top; press gently onto surface. Cool completely in pan on wire rack. Cut into bars.

Makes about 3 dozen bars

Toffee Topping: In small saucepan, over medium heat, combine 2/3 cup butter and 1/3 cup packed light brown sugar. Cook, stirring constantly, until mixture comes to a boil. Continue boiling and stirring 30 seconds; use immediately.

Quick and Easy Nutty Cheese Bars

CHOCOLATE CHERRY BROWNIES

1 jar (16 ounces) maraschino cherries
2/3 cup (1 stick plus 3 tablespoons) margarine
1 package (6 ounces) semi-sweet chocolate pieces (1 cup), divided
1 cup sugar
1 teaspoon vanilla
2 eggs
1 1/4 cups all-purpose flour
3/4 cup QUAKER® Oats (Quick or Old Fashioned, uncooked)
1 teaspoon baking powder
1/4 teaspoon salt (optional)
1/2 cup chopped nuts (optional)
2 teaspoons vegetable shortening

Preheat oven to 350°F. Lightly grease 13×9-inch baking pan. Drain cherries; reserve 12 and chop remainder. In large saucepan over low heat, melt margarine and 1/2 cup chocolate pieces, stirring until smooth. Remove from heat; cool slightly. Add sugar and vanilla. Beat in eggs, one at a time. Add combined flour, oats, baking powder and salt. Stir in chopped cherries and nuts. Spread into prepared pan.

Bake about 25 minutes or until brownies pull away from sides of pan. Cool completely in pan on wire rack.

Cut reserved cherries in half; place evenly on top of brownies. In saucepan over low heat, melt remaining 1/2 cup chocolate pieces and vegetable shortening, stirring constantly until smooth.* Drizzle over brownies; cut into about 2 1/2-inch squares. Store tightly covered.

Makes about 2 dozen bars

*Microwave Directions: Place chocolate pieces and shortening in microwaveable bowl. Microwave at HIGH 1 to 1 1/2 minutes, stirring after 1 minute.

PECAN MINCE BARS

1 1/2 cups plus 3 tablespoons unsifted all-purpose flour, divided
1/3 cup confectioners' sugar
3/4 cup cold margarine or butter
4 eggs, beaten
1 (9-ounce) package NONE SUCH® Condensed Mincemeat, crumbled
1 cup chopped pecans
1/3 cup firmly packed light brown sugar
1 teaspoon grated lemon rind
1/2 teaspoon baking powder
Pecan halves (optional)

Continued

Preheat oven to 350°F. Lightly grease 13×9-inch baking pan. In small mixer bowl, combine *1½ cups* flour, confectioners' sugar and margarine; mix until crumbly. Press onto bottom of prepared pan. Bake 20 minutes.

Meanwhile, in large bowl, combine remaining *3 tablespoons* flour, eggs, mincemeat, chopped pecans, brown sugar, lemon rind and baking powder; beat well. Spread evenly over baked crust. Bake 20 to 25 minutes more or until set. Cool in pan on wire rack. Garnish with pecan halves, if desired. Cut into bars. Store loosely covered at room temperature.

Makes 2 to 3 dozen bars

ORANGE PUMPKIN BARS

BARS

1½ cups all-purpose flour
1 teaspoon baking powder
1 teaspoon pumpkin pie spice
½ teaspoon baking soda
½ teaspoon salt
1 cup canned solid-packed pumpkin (not pumpkin pie filling)
¾ cup granulated sugar
⅔ cup CRISCO® Oil
2 eggs
¼ cup firmly packed light brown sugar
2 tablespoons orange juice
½ cup chopped nuts
½ cup raisins

ICING

1½ cups powdered sugar
2 tablespoons orange juice
2 tablespoons butter or margarine, softened
½ teaspoon grated orange peel

1. Preheat oven to 350°F. Grease and flour 12×8-inch baking dish.

2. For bars, combine flour, baking powder, pumpkin pie spice, baking soda and salt in medium mixing bowl. Combine pumpkin, granulated sugar, Crisco® Oil, eggs, brown sugar and orange juice in large mixing bowl. Beat at low speed of electric mixer until blended, scraping bowl constantly. Add flour mixture. Beat at medium speed until smooth, scraping bowl frequently. Stir in nuts and raisins. Pour into prepared pan.

3. Bake about 35 minutes or until center springs back when touched lightly. Cool completely on wire rack.

4. For icing, combine powdered sugar, orange juice, butter and orange peel. Beat at medium speed of electric mixer until smooth. Spread over cooled bars.

Makes 24 bars

Almond Apricot Bars

ALMOND APRICOT BARS

- 2/3 cup dried apricots
- 1 1/3 cups all-purpose flour, divided
- 1/4 cup granulated sugar
- 1/3 cup cold butter
- 1 cup sliced natural almonds, toasted and divided
- 2 eggs
- 1 cup packed brown sugar
- 1/2 teaspoon vanilla extract
- 1/4 teaspoon almond extract
- 1/4 teaspoon grated lemon peel
- 1 tablespoon lemon juice
- 1/2 teaspoon baking powder

Continued

Preheat oven to 350°F. Place apricots in small saucepan; cover with water and bring to a boil. Simmer apricots 10 minutes; drain, chop and set aside. Blend 1 cup flour with granulated sugar. Cut in butter until mixture resembles cornmeal. Stir in ½ cup almonds. Pat into ungreased 9-inch square pan.

Bake 20 minutes. Beat eggs and brown sugar until sugar is dissolved. Blend in vanilla and almond extracts, lemon peel and lemon juice. Blend remaining ⅓ cup flour with baking powder. Fold into egg mixture. Stir in chopped apricots. Pour over base. Sprinkle with remaining ½ cup almonds. Return to oven; bake 25 minutes. Cool in pan on wire rack. Cut into bars.

Makes 2 dozen bars

Favorite recipe from Almond Board of California

PUMPKIN PECAN PIE BARS

- **1 cup firmly packed brown sugar**
- **½ cup margarine or butter, softened**
- **1½ cups unsifted all-purpose flour**
- **1 cup rolled oats**
- **1 teaspoon baking powder**
- **1 teaspoon salt**
- **1 (16-ounce) can pumpkin (about 2 cups)**
- **1 (14-ounce) can EAGLE® Brand Sweetened Condensed Milk (NOT evaporated milk)**
- **2 eggs, beaten**
- **2 teaspoons pumpkin pie spice**
- **1½ teaspoons vanilla extract**
- **1 cup chopped pecans**
- **Confectioners' sugar (optional)**

Preheat oven to 350°F. In large mixer bowl, beat sugar and margarine until fluffy; add flour, oats, baking powder and *½ teaspoon* salt. Mix until crumbly. Reserve ½ cup crumb mixture. Press remaining crumb mixture on bottom of ungreased 15×10-inch baking pan. Bake 20 minutes.

Meanwhile, in medium bowl, combine pumpkin, sweetened condensed milk, eggs, pumpkin pie spice, vanilla and remaining *½ teaspoon* salt. Spread over crust. In small bowl, combine reserved crumb mixture with pecans; sprinkle over pumpkin mixture. Bake 30 to 35 minutes or until set. Cool in pan on wire rack. Sprinkle with confectioners' sugar, if desired. Cut into bars. Store covered in refrigerator.

Makes 3 to 4 dozen bars

ROCKY ROAD BROWNIES

½ cup butter or margarine
½ cup unsweetened cocoa
1 cup sugar
1 egg
½ cup all-purpose flour
¼ cup buttermilk
1 teaspoon vanilla
1 cup miniature marshmallows
1 cup coarsely chopped walnuts
1 cup (6 ounces) semisweet chocolate chips

Preheat oven to 350°F. Lightly grease an 8-inch square pan. Combine butter and cocoa in medium-sized heavy saucepan over low heat, stirring constantly until smooth. Remove from heat; stir in sugar, egg, flour, buttermilk and vanilla. Mix until smooth. Spread batter evenly in prepared pan. Bake 25 minutes or until center feels dry. (Do not overbake or brownies will be dry.) Remove from oven; sprinkle marshmallows, walnuts and chocolate chips over the top. Return to oven for 3 to 5 minutes or just until topping is warmed enough to melt together. Cool in pan on wire rack. Cut into 2-inch squares.

Makes 16 brownies

RICH LEMON BARS

1½ cups plus 3 tablespoons unsifted all-purpose flour
½ cup confectioners' sugar
¾ cup cold margarine or butter
4 eggs, slightly beaten
1½ cups granulated sugar
1 teaspoon baking powder
½ cup REALEMON® Lemon Juice from Concentrate
Additional confectioners' sugar

Preheat oven to 350°F. Lightly grease 13×9-inch baking pan. In medium bowl, combine *1½ cups* flour and confectioners' sugar; cut in margarine until crumbly. Press onto bottom of prepared pan. Bake 15 minutes.

Meanwhile, in large bowl, combine eggs, granulated sugar, baking powder, ReaLemon® brand and remaining *3 tablespoons* flour; mix well. Pour over baked crust; bake 20 to 25 minutes or until golden brown. Cool. Cut into bars. Sprinkle with additional confectioners' sugar. Store covered in refrigerator; serve at room temperature.

Makes 2 to 3 dozen bars

Lemon Pecan Bars: Omit 3 tablespoons flour in lemon mixture. Sprinkle ¾ cup finely chopped pecans over top of lemon mixture. Bake as directed.

Coconut Lemon Bars: Omit 3 tablespoons flour in lemon mixture. Sprinkle ¾ cup flaked coconut over top of lemon mixture. Bake as directed.

Rocky Road Brownies

APPLESAUCE FRUITCAKE BARS

- 1 (14-ounce) can EAGLE® Brand Sweetened Condensed Milk (NOT evaporated milk)
- 2 eggs
- 1/4 cup margarine or butter, melted
- 2 teaspoons vanilla extract
- 3 cups biscuit baking mix
- 1 (15-ounce) jar applesauce
- 1 cup chopped dates
- 1 (6-ounce) container green candied cherries, chopped
- 1 (6-ounce) container red candied cherries, chopped
- 1 cup chopped nuts
- 1 cup raisins
- Confectioners' sugar

Preheat oven to 325°F. Grease well and flour 15×10-inch baking pan. In large mixer bowl, beat sweetened condensed milk, eggs, margarine and vanilla. Stir in remaining ingredients except confectioners' sugar; mix well. Spread evenly into prepared pan.

Bake 35 to 40 minutes or until wooden pick inserted in center comes out clean. Cool in pan on wire rack. Sprinkle with confectioners' sugar. Cut into bars. Store tightly covered at room temperature.

Makes 3 to 4 dozen bars

Applesauce Fruitcake Bars

ALMOND DREAM BARS

18 graham crackers, divided
3/4 cup firmly packed brown sugar
1/2 cup butter or margarine
1/2 cup *undiluted* CARNATION® Evaporated Milk
1 cup graham cracker crumbs
1 cup sliced almonds, divided
1 cup flaked coconut
1/2 cup chopped dried apricots
Almond Icing (recipe follows)

Butter 8-inch square dish. Line bottom with 9 of the graham crackers. In medium saucepan, combine brown sugar, butter and evaporated milk. Cook over medium heat, stirring constantly, until mixture comes to a full boil. Remove from heat. Immediately stir in graham cracker crumbs, *3/4 cup* almonds, coconut and apricots. Spread apricot mixture evenly over graham crackers in dish. Top with remaining 9 graham crackers. Press down firmly. Spread with Almond Icing. Sprinkle with remaining 1/4 cup almonds. Chill until firm. Cut into bars. *Makes 32 bars*

Almond Icing: In medium bowl, blend 1 1/2 cups sifted powdered sugar with 2 tablespoons softened butter or margarine. Add 2 tablespoons *undiluted* CARNATION® Evaporated Milk and 1/2 teaspoon almond extract. Beat until smooth.

BANANA-DATE BARS

3 ripe, medium DOLE® Bananas, peeled
1/2 cup margarine, softened
1 cup brown sugar, packed
2 eggs
2 cups all-purpose flour
1 teaspoon baking soda
1 teaspoon ground cinnamon
1/2 teaspoon baking powder
1/2 teaspoon ground nutmeg
1/4 teaspoon salt
1 cup DOLE® Chopped Dates
1 cup chopped walnuts
Powdered sugar

Preheat oven to 350°F. Grease 13×9-inch pan. Purée 1 banana in blender or food processor, making 1/2 cup purée. Dice remaining 2 bananas. Cream margarine and brown sugar until light and fluffy. Beat in eggs. Beat in puréed banana. Combine dry ingredients; beat into creamed mixture until well blended. Fold in dates, nuts and diced bananas. Turn batter into prepared pan.

Bake 25 minutes. Cool in pan on wire rack. Sprinkle with powdered sugar. Cut into bars. *Makes 2 dozen bars*

BLONDE BRICKLE BROWNIES

- 1⅓ cups all-purpose flour
- ½ teaspoon baking powder
- ¼ teaspoon salt
- 2 eggs, room temperature
- ½ cup granulated sugar
- ½ cup packed brown sugar
- ⅓ cup butter or margarine, melted
- 1 teaspoon vanilla
- ¼ teaspoon almond extract
- 1 package (6 ounces) BITS 'O BRICKLE®, divided
- ½ cup chopped pecans (optional)

Preheat oven to 350°F. Grease 8-inch square baking pan. Combine flour, baking powder and salt; set aside. Beat eggs well. Gradually add granulated and brown sugar; beat until thick and creamy. Add melted butter, vanilla and almond extract. Gently stir in flour mixture until moistened. Fold in ⅔ cup of the Bits 'O Brickle® and nuts. Pour into prepared pan.

Bake 30 minutes. Remove from oven and immediately sprinkle remaining Bits 'O Brickle® over top. Cool completely in pan on wire rack before cutting.

Makes 16 generous bars

HERSHEY®S PREMIUM DOUBLE CHOCOLATE BROWNIES

- ¾ cup HERSHEY®S Cocoa
- ½ teaspoon baking soda
- ⅔ cup butter or margarine, melted and divided
- ½ cup boiling water
- 2 cups sugar
- 2 eggs, slightly beaten
- 1⅓ cups all-purpose flour
- 1 teaspoon vanilla extract
- ¼ teaspoon salt
- 2 cups (12-ounce package) HERSHEY®S Semi-Sweet Chocolate Chips
- ½ cup coarsely chopped nuts (optional)

Preheat oven to 350°F. Grease 13×9-inch baking pan. In bowl, stir together cocoa and baking soda; blend in ⅓ cup melted butter. Add boiling water; stir until mixture thickens. Stir in sugar, eggs and remaining ⅓ cup melted butter; stir until smooth. Add flour, vanilla and salt; blend well. Stir in chocolate chips and nuts, if desired. Pour into prepared pan. Bake 35 to 40 minutes or until brownies begin to pull away from sides of pan. Cool completely in pan on wire rack. Cut into squares.

Makes about 3 dozen bars

Blonde Brickle Brownies

A Star &

PRUNE BARS

- 2 cups all-purpose flour
- 1 cup sugar
- 1 teaspoon salt
- 1/2 teaspoon baking soda
- 3/4 cup cold butter or margarine
- 1 1/2 cups shredded or flaked coconut
- 1 cup chopped nuts (walnuts, pecans or almonds)
- 1 can SOLO® *or* BAKER® Prune or Date Filling

Preheat oven to 400°F. Grease 13×9-inch baking pan. Combine flour, sugar, salt and baking soda in medium bowl and stir until blended. Cut in butter until mixture resembles coarse crumbs. Add coconut and chopped nuts; stir until well mixed. Reserve 2 cups of the flour-coconut mixture. Press remaining mixture into bottom of prepared pan.

Bake 10 minutes. Remove from oven and spread prune filling over baked crust. Sprinkle reserved flour-coconut mixture over filling. Bake 15 minutes more or until top is golden brown. Cool completely in pan on wire rack. Cut into bars. *Makes 3 dozen bars*

Prune Bars

LINZER BARS

This fancy dessert treat is filled with jam and crisscrossed with a lattice design.

- **3/4 cup butter or margarine, softened**
- **1/2 cup sugar**
- **1 egg**
- **1/2 teaspoon grated lemon peel**
- **1/2 teaspoon ground cinnamon**
- **1/4 teaspoon salt**
- **1/8 teaspoon ground cloves**
- **2 cups all-purpose flour**
- **1 cup DIAMOND® Walnuts, finely chopped or ground**
- **1 cup raspberry or apricot jam**

Preheat oven to 325°F. Grease 9-inch square pan. In large bowl, cream butter, sugar, egg, lemon peel, cinnamon, salt and cloves. Blend in flour and walnuts. Set aside about 1/4 of the dough for lattice top. Pat remaining dough into bottom and about 1/2 inch up sides of pan. Spread with jam. Make pencil-shaped strips of remaining dough, rolling against floured board with palms of hands. Arrange in lattice pattern over top, pressing ends against dough on sides.

Bake 45 minutes or until lightly browned. Cool in pan on wire rack. Cut into bars.

Makes 2 dozen small bars

HERSHEY®S CHOCOLATE CHIP BLONDIES

- **3/4 cup packed light brown sugar**
- **6 tablespoons butter or margarine, softened**
- **1 egg**
- **1 tablespoon milk**
- **1 teaspoon vanilla extract**
- **1 cup all-purpose flour**
- **1/2 teaspoon baking soda**
- **1/8 teaspoon salt**
- **2 cups (12-ounce package) HERSHEY®S Semi-Sweet Chocolate Chips**
- **1/2 cup coarsely chopped nuts (optional)**

Preheat oven to 350°F. Grease 9-inch square baking pan. In large mixer bowl, beat brown sugar and butter until light and fluffy. Add egg, milk and vanilla; beat well. Stir together flour, baking soda and salt; add to butter mixture. Stir in chocolate chips and nuts, if desired; spread in prepared pan. Bake 20 to 25 minutes or until lightly browned. Cool completely in pan on wire rack. Cut into bars.

Makes about 1½ dozen bars

CHOCOLATE PECAN PIE BARS

1⅓ cups all-purpose flour
½ cup plus 2 tablespoons packed light brown sugar, divided
½ cup butter or margarine
2 eggs
½ cup light corn syrup
¼ cup HERSHEY®S Cocoa
2 tablespoons butter or margarine, melted
1 teaspoon vanilla extract
⅛ teaspoon salt
1 cup coarsely chopped pecans

Preheat oven to 350°F. In medium bowl stir together flour and 2 tablespoons brown sugar. Cut in ½ cup butter until mixture resembles coarse crumbs; press onto bottom and about 1 inch up sides of 9-inch square baking pan.

Bake 10 to 12 minutes or until set. With back of spoon, lightly press crust into corners and against sides of pan.

Meanwhile, in small bowl lightly beat eggs, corn syrup, remaining ½ cup brown sugar, cocoa, melted butter, vanilla and salt. Stir in pecans. Pour mixture over warm crust.

Return to oven. Bake 25 minutes more or until pecan filling is set. Cool completely in pan on wire rack. Cut into bars. *Makes 16 bars*

BAR COOKIE CRUST

MAZOLA® No Stick Cooking Spray
2½ cups all-purpose flour
1 cup cold MAZOLA® Margarine, cut in pieces
½ cup confectioners' sugar
¼ teaspoon salt

Preheat oven to 350°F. Spray 15×10×1-inch baking pan with cooking spray. In large bowl with mixer at medium speed, beat flour, margarine, sugar and salt until mixture resembles coarse crumbs; press firmly and evenly into prepared pan.

Bake 20 minutes or until golden brown. Top with desired filling. Finish baking according to individual recipe directions.

Chocolate-Drizzled Peanut Bars

CHOCOLATE-DRIZZLED PEANUT BARS

Bar Cookie Crust (see page 70)
1/2 cup packed brown sugar
1/3 cup KARO® Light Corn Syrup
1/4 cup MAZOLA® Margarine
1/4 cup heavy cream
1 teaspoon vanilla
1/4 teaspoon lemon juice
1 1/2 cups coarsely chopped roasted peanuts
Chocolate Glaze (recipe follows)

Preheat oven to 350°F. Prepare Bar Cookie Crust. In medium saucepan combine brown sugar, corn syrup, margarine and cream. Bring to boil over medium heat; remove from heat. Stir in vanilla and lemon juice, then peanuts. Pour over hot crust; spread evenly.

Bake 15 to 20 minutes or until set. Cool completely on wire rack. Drizzle with Chocolate Glaze; cool before cutting. *Makes about 5 dozen bars*

Chocolate Glaze: In small heavy saucepan over low heat, combine 2/3 cup semisweet chocolate chips and 1 tablespoon MAZOLA® Margarine; stir until melted and smooth.

CHOCOLATE CREAM CHEESE SUGAR COOKIE BARS

1 box (15 ounces) golden sugar cookie mix
1 package (8 ounces) cream cheese, softened
1/4 cup butter or margarine, softened
1/4 cup HERSHEY®S Cocoa
1/2 cup granulated sugar
1 egg
1 teaspoon vanilla extract
Powdered sugar (optional)

Preheat oven to 350°F. Mix cookie dough according to package directions; spread in 9-inch square baking pan. In small mixer bowl, beat cream cheese and butter until light and fluffy. Stir together cocoa and granulated sugar; add to butter mixture. Add egg and vanilla; beat until smooth. Spread cream cheese mixture over cookie batter.

Bake 40 minutes or until no imprint remains when touched lightly. Cool completely in pan on wire rack. Sprinkle powdered sugar over top, if desired. Cut into bars. Cover; refrigerate. *Makes about 16 bars*

ALMOND SHORTBREAD

Rich, delicate shortbread dough is laced with crisp, toasted chips of sliced almonds to add new flavor and texture to a popular classic.

1 cup all-purpose flour
1/2 cup sifted powdered sugar
1/4 cup cornstarch
1/2 cup butter, softened
1/4 teaspoon vanilla extract
1/4 teaspoon almond extract
1/2 cup BLUE DIAMOND® Sliced, Natural Almonds, toasted and lightly crushed

Preheat oven to 350°F. In food processor, combine flour, sugar and cornstarch. With on-off bursts, add butter, vanilla and almond extracts and almonds until mixture just forms a ball. (To prepare without a food processor, combine flour, powdered sugar and cornstarch. With fingertips, work butter into flour mixture until mixture resembles coarse cornmeal. Add vanilla and almond extracts and almonds and form dough into ball.)

Pat dough into ungreased 8-inch round pie pan; smooth top. Prick top with fork. With knife, score into eight wedges. Decorate edge by indenting with tines of fork. Bake 25 minutes or until firm. Cut into wedges. *Makes 8 wedges*

Chocolate Cream Cheese Sugar Cookie Bars

MINT CHOCOLATE TRUFFLE BARS

BASE
¾ cup (1½ sticks) butter, softened
1½ cups all-purpose flour
½ cup sugar
2 tablespoons NESTLÉ® Toll House Baking Cocoa

TOPPING
One 10-ounce package (1½ cups) NESTLÉ® Toll House® mint-chocolate morsels
½ cup (1 stick) butter
4 eggs
¼ cup sugar
2 tablespoons all-purpose flour
1 teaspoon vanilla extract
Confectioners' sugar

Base: Preheat oven to 350°F. In small mixer bowl, beat ingredients for base until a soft dough forms; spread dough in ungreased 13×9-inch baking pan. Bake 8 to 9 minutes or until crust is barely set.

Topping: In small saucepan over very low heat, melt Nestlé® Toll House® mint-chocolate morsels and butter, stirring constantly; remove from heat.

In small mixer bowl, beat eggs and sugar until light and fluffy, about 3 minutes. At low speed, beat in flour, vanilla extract and melted chocolate. Pour over crust.

Bake 18 minutes or *just* until toothpick inserted in center comes out clean. (Topping may puff and crack, but will flatten as it cools.) Cool in pan on wire rack. Sprinkle with confectioners' sugar. Cut into 1½-inch squares.

Makes about 4 dozen bars

CRANBERRY WALNUT BARS

Bar Cookie Crust (see page 70)
4 eggs
1⅓ cups KARO® Light or Dark Corn Syrup
1 cup sugar
3 tablespoons MAZOLA® Margarine, melted
2 cups coarsely chopped fresh or frozen cranberries
1 cup chopped walnuts

Preheat oven to 350°F. Prepare Bar Cookie Crust. In large bowl beat eggs, corn syrup, sugar and margarine until well blended. Stir in cranberries and walnuts. Pour over hot crust; spread evenly. Bake 25 to 30 minutes or until set. Cool completely on wire rack before cutting.

Makes 4 dozen bars

CHOCOLATE PEANUT BUTTER SQUARES

1½ cups chocolate-covered graham cracker crumbs (about 17 crackers)
3 tablespoons PARKAY® Margarine, melted
1 (8-ounce) package PHILADELPHIA BRAND® Cream Cheese, softened
½ cup chunk style peanut butter
1 cup powdered sugar
¼ cup BAKER'S® Semi-Sweet Real Chocolate Chips
1 teaspoon shortening

Preheat oven to 350°F.

Stir together crumbs and margarine in small bowl. Press onto bottom of 9-inch square baking pan. Bake 10 minutes. Cool.

Beat cream cheese, peanut butter and sugar in small mixing bowl at medium speed with electric mixer until well blended. Spread over crust.

Melt chocolate chips with shortening in small saucepan over low heat, stirring until smooth. Drizzle over cream cheese mixture. Chill 6 hours or overnight. Cut into squares. *Makes about 1 dozen bars*

Microwave Tip: Microwave chocolate chips and shortening in small microwave-safe bowl on HIGH 1 to 2 minutes or until chocolate begins to melt, stirring every minute. Stir until chocolate is melted.

Chocolate Peanut Butter Squares

Fancy Cookies

These eye-catching cookies are as delectable as they look! The sensational results are worth the extra time it takes to make them.

BRANDY LACE COOKIES

Reserve these crisp, intriguing cookies for a special occasion. If time is limited, curling the cookies is optional.

1/4 cup sugar
1/4 cup MAZOLA® Margarine
1/4 cup KARO® Light or Dark Corn Syrup
1/2 cup all-purpose flour
1/4 cup very finely chopped pecans or walnuts
2 tablespoons brandy
Melted white and/or semisweet chocolate (optional)

Preheat oven to 350°F. Lightly grease and flour cookie sheets. In small saucepan combine sugar, margarine and corn syrup. Bring to boil over medium heat, stirring constantly. Remove from heat. Stir in flour, pecans and brandy. Drop 12 evenly spaced half teaspoonfuls of batter onto prepared cookie sheets.

Bake 6 minutes or until golden. Cool 1 to 2 minutes or until cookies can be lifted but are still warm and pliable; remove with spatula. Curl around handle of wooden spoon; slide off when crisp. If cookies harden before curling, return to oven to soften. Drizzle with melted chocolate, if desired.

Makes 4 to 5 dozen cookies

Top: Brandy Lace Cookies
Bottom: Kentucky Bourbon Pecan Tarts (page 83)

Top: Honey-Ginger Bourbon Balls (page 46)
Bottom: Chocolate-Frosted Lebkuchen

CHOCOLATE-FROSTED LEBKUCHEN

Lebkuchen are holiday favorites in Germany.

- 4 eggs
- 1 cup sugar
- 1½ cups all-purpose flour
- 1 cup (6 ounces) pulverized almonds*
- ⅓ cup candied lemon peel, finely chopped
- ⅓ cup candied orange peel, finely chopped
- 1½ teaspoons ground cinnamon
- 1 teaspoon grated lemon peel
- ½ teaspoon ground cardamom
- ½ teaspoon ground nutmeg
- ¼ teaspoon ground cloves
- Bittersweet Glaze (recipe follows)

Continued

In large bowl of electric mixer, combine eggs and sugar. Beat at high speed for 10 minutes. Meanwhile, in separate bowl, combine flour, almonds, candied lemon and orange peels, cinnamon, lemon peel, cardamom, nutmeg and cloves. Blend in egg mixture, stirring until evenly mixed. Cover; refrigerate 12 hours or overnight.

Preheat oven to 350°F. Grease cookie sheets and dust with flour or line with parchment paper. Drop dough by rounded teaspoonfuls 2 inches apart onto prepared cookie sheets.

Bake 8 to 10 minutes or until just barely browned. Do not overbake. Remove to wire racks. While cookies bake, prepare Bittersweet Glaze. Spread over tops of warm cookies using pastry brush. Cool until glaze is set. Store in airtight container. *Makes about 5 dozen cookies*

*To pulverize almonds, place in food processor or blender. Process until thoroughly ground with a dry, not pasty, texture.

Bittersweet Glaze: Melt 3 chopped squares (1 ounce each) bittersweet or semisweet chocolate and 1 tablespoon butter or margarine in small bowl over hot water. Stir until smooth.

MOIST PUMPKIN COOKIES

- **½ cup butter or margarine, softened**
- **1 cup packed brown sugar**
- **½ cup granulated sugar**
- **1½ cups canned pumpkin (not pumpkin pie filling)**
- **1 egg**
- **1 teaspoon vanilla extract**
- **2¼ cups all-purpose flour**
- **1¼ teaspoons ground cinnamon**
- **1 teaspoon baking powder**
- **½ teaspoon baking soda**
- **½ teaspoon salt**
- **½ teaspoon ground nutmeg**
- **¾ cup raisins**
- **½ cup chopped walnuts**
- **Powdered Sugar Glaze (recipe follows)**

Preheat oven to 350°F. Beat butter and sugars in large bowl until creamy. Beat in pumpkin, egg and vanilla until light and fluffy. Mix in flour, cinnamon, baking powder, baking soda, salt and nutmeg until blended. Stir in raisins and walnuts. Drop heaping tablespoonfuls of dough 2 inches apart onto ungreased cookie sheets.

Bake 12 to 15 minutes until set. Cool 2 minutes on cookie sheets. Remove to wire racks; cool completely. Drizzle Powdered Sugar Glaze onto cookies. Let glaze set. Store between layers of waxed paper in airtight containers. *Makes about 3½ dozen cookies*

Powdered Sugar Glaze: Combine 1 cup powdered sugar and 2 tablespoons milk in small bowl until well blended.

ALMOND RICE MADELEINES

Vegetable oil cooking spray
1 cup whole blanched almonds, lightly toasted
1½ cups sugar
¾ cup flaked coconut
3 cups cooked rice, chilled
3 egg whites
Fresh raspberries (optional)
Frozen nondairy whipped topping, thawed (optional)
Powdered sugar (optional)

Preheat oven to 350°F. Coat madeleine pans* with vegetable oil cooking spray. Place almonds in food processor fitted with knife blade; process until finely ground. Add sugar and coconut to processor; process until coconut is finely minced. Add rice; pulse to blend. Add egg whites; pulse to blend. Spoon mixture evenly into madeleine pans, filling to tops.

Bake 25 to 30 minutes or until lightly browned. Cool completely in pans on wire rack. Cover and refrigerate 2 hours or until serving time. Run a sharp knife around each madeleine shell and gently remove from pan. Invert onto serving plates; serve with raspberries and whipped topping, if desired. Sprinkle with powdered sugar, if desired.

Makes about 3 dozen madeleines

*You may substitute miniature muffin pans for madeleine pans, if desired.

Favorite recipe from USA Rice Council

MINI MORSEL MERINGUE WREATHS

2 egg whites
¼ teaspoon cream of tartar
⅓ cup sugar
½ cup (¼ of 12-ounce package) NESTLÉ® Toll House® semi-sweet chocolate mini morsels
One 3-ounce package candied cherries, quartered

Preheat oven to 275°F. In small mixer bowl, beat egg whites and cream of tartar until soft peaks form. Gradually add sugar; beat until stiff peaks form. Fold in Nestlé® Toll House® semi-sweet chocolate mini morsels. Spoon into pastry bag fitted with plain #7 pastry tip. Pipe 2-inch circles onto parchment paper-lined cookie sheets. Top each wreath with two candied cherry pieces. Bake 20 minutes. Turn oven off; let stand in oven 30 minutes with door ajar. Cool; peel off paper. Store in airtight container.

Makes 2½ dozen cookies

Almond Rice Madeleines

CHOCOLATE PISTACHIO FINGERS

Both ends of these buttery, finger-shaped cookies are dipped into melted chocolate. Then, for an elegant finish, the chocolate ends are covered with chopped pistachios.

- **¾ cup butter or margarine, softened**
- **⅓ cup sugar**
- **3 ounces (about ⅓ cup) almond paste**
- **1 egg yolk**
- **1⅔ cups all-purpose flour**
- **1 cup (6 ounces) semisweet chocolate chips**
- **½ cup finely chopped natural pistachios**

Preheat oven to 350°F. Line cookie sheets with parchment paper or lightly grease and dust with flour. Cream butter and sugar in large bowl until blended. Add almond paste and egg yolk; beat until light. Blend in flour to make a smooth dough. (If dough is too soft to handle, cover and refrigerate until firm.)

Turn out onto lightly floured board. Divide into 8 equal pieces; divide each piece in half. Roll each half into a 12-inch rope; cut each rope into 2-inch lengths. Place 2 inches apart on prepared cookie sheets.

Bake 10 to 12 minutes or until edges just begin to brown. Remove to wire racks to cool.

Melt chocolate chips in small bowl over hot water. Stir until smooth. Dip both ends of cookies about ½ inch into melted chocolate, then dip the chocolate ends into pistachios. Place on waxed paper; let stand until chocolate is set.

Makes about 8 dozen cookies

Chocolate Pistachio Fingers;
Chocolate-Dipped Oat Cookies (page 4)

KENTUCKY BOURBON PECAN TARTS

These bite-size Southern favorites are ideal for a dessert buffet. For added convenience, prepare ahead and keep frozen for up to two weeks.

Cream Cheese Pastry (recipe follows)
2 eggs
½ cup granulated sugar
½ cup KARO® Light or Dark Corn Syrup
2 tablespoons bourbon
1 tablespoon MAZOLA® Margarine, melted
½ teaspoon vanilla
1 cup chopped pecans
Confectioners' sugar (optional)

Preheat oven to 350°F. Prepare Cream Cheese Pastry. Divide dough in half; set aside one half. On floured surface roll out pastry to ⅛-inch thickness. *If necessary, add small amount of flour to keep pastry from sticking.* Cut into 12 (2¼-inch) rounds. Press evenly into bottoms and up sides of 1¾-inch muffin pan cups. Repeat with remaining pastry. Refrigerate.

In medium bowl, slightly beat eggs. Stir in granulated sugar, corn syrup, bourbon, margarine and vanilla until well blended. Spoon 1 heaping teaspoon pecans into each pastry-lined cup; top with 1 tablespoon corn syrup mixture.

Bake 20 to 25 minutes or until lightly browned and toothpick inserted into center comes out clean. Cool in pans 5 minutes. Remove; cool completely on wire rack. If desired, sprinkle with confectioners' sugar.

Makes about 2 dozen tarts

CREAM CHEESE PASTRY

1 cup all-purpose flour
¾ teaspoon baking powder
Pinch salt
½ cup MAZOLA® Margarine, softened
1 package (3 ounces) cream cheese, softened
2 teaspoons sugar

In small bowl combine flour, baking powder and salt. In large bowl mix margarine, cream cheese and sugar until well combined. Stir in flour mixture until well blended. Press firmly into ball with hands.

DOUBLE-DIPPED HAZELNUT CRISPS

¾ cup semisweet chocolate chips
1¼ cups all-purpose flour
¾ cup powdered sugar
⅔ cup whole hazelnuts, toasted, hulled and pulverized*
¼ teaspoon instant espresso coffee powder
Dash salt
½ cup butter or margarine, softened
2 teaspoons vanilla
4 squares (1 ounce each) bittersweet or semisweet chocolate
4 ounces white chocolate
2 teaspoons shortening, divided

Preheat oven to 350°F. Lightly grease cookie sheets or line with parchment paper. Melt chocolate chips in top of double boiler over hot, not boiling, water. Remove from heat; cool. Blend flour, sugar, hazelnuts, coffee powder and salt in large bowl. Blend in butter, melted chocolate and vanilla until dough is stiff but smooth. (If dough is too soft to handle, cover and refrigerate until firm.)

Roll out dough, one fourth at a time, to ⅛-inch thickness on lightly floured surface. Cut out with 2-inch scalloped round cutter. Place 2 inches apart on prepared cookie sheets.

Bake 8 minutes or until not quite firm. (Cookies should not brown. They will puff up during baking and then fall again.) Remove to wire racks to cool.

Place bittersweet and white chocolates in separate small bowls. Add 1 teaspoon shortening to each bowl. Place bowls over hot water; stir until chocolates are melted and smooth. Dip cookies, one at a time, halfway into bittersweet chocolate. Place on waxed paper; refrigerate until chocolate is set. Dip other halves of cookies into white chocolate; refrigerate until set. Store cookies in airtight container in cool place. (If cookies are frozen, chocolate may discolor.)

Makes about 4 dozen cookies

*To pulverize hazelnuts, place in food processor or blender. Process until thoroughly ground with a dry, not pasty, texture.

Double-Dipped Hazelnut Crisps; Pecan Florentines (page 86)

PECAN FLORENTINES

Florentines are lacy confections that require a bit more skill to prepare than the average drop cookie. When baked on foil as directed, they are much easier to handle.

3/4 cup pecan halves, pulverized*
1/2 cup all-purpose flour
1/3 cup packed brown sugar
1/4 cup light corn syrup
1/4 cup butter or margarine
2 tablespoons milk
1/3 cup semisweet chocolate chips

Preheat oven to 350°F. Line cookie sheets with foil; lightly grease foil. Combine pecans and flour in small bowl. Combine brown sugar, syrup, butter and milk in medium saucepan. Stir over medium heat until mixture comes to a boil. Remove from heat; stir in flour mixture. Drop batter by teaspoonfuls about 3 inches apart onto prepared cookie sheets.

Bake 10 to 12 minutes or until lacy and golden brown. (Cookies are soft when hot, but become crisp as they cool.) Remove cookies by lifting foil from cookie sheet; set foil on flat, heat-proof surface. Cool cookies completely on foil.

Place chocolate chips in small heavy-duty plastic bag; close securely. Set bag in bowl of hot water until chips are melted, being careful not to let any water into bag. (Knead bag lightly to check that chips are completely melted.) Pat bag dry. With scissors, snip off a small corner from one side of bag. Squeeze melted chocolate over cookies to decorate. Let stand until chocolate is set. Peel cookies off foil. *Makes about 3 dozen cookies*

*To pulverize pecans, place in food processor or blender. Process until thoroughly ground with a dry, not pasty, texture.

PINWHEEL COOKIES

1/2 cup BUTTER FLAVOR CRISCO® all-vegetable shortening
1/3 cup plus 1 tablespoon butter, softened and divided
2 egg yolks
1/2 teaspoon vanilla
1 package DUNCAN HINES® Moist Deluxe Fudge Marble Cake Mix

1. Combine shortening, 1/3 cup butter, egg yolks and vanilla in large bowl. Mix at low speed of electric mixer until blended. Set aside cocoa packet from cake mix. Gradually add cake mix. Blend well.

Continued

2. Divide dough in half. Add cocoa packet and remaining 1 tablespoon butter to *half* the dough. Knead until well blended and chocolate colored.

3. Roll out yellow dough between two pieces of waxed paper into 18×12×1/8-inch rectangle. Repeat for chocolate dough. Remove top pieces of waxed paper from chocolate and yellow dough. Lay yellow dough directly on top of chocolate. Remove remaining waxed paper. Roll up jelly-roll fashion, beginning at wide side. Cover and refrigerate 2 hours.

4. Preheat oven to 350°F. Grease baking sheets. Cut dough into 1/8-inch slices. Bake 9 to 11 minutes or until lightly browned. Cool 5 minutes on baking sheets. Remove to wire racks to cool completely.

Makes about 3½ dozen cookies

Tip: You can use DUNCAN HINES® Moist Deluxe White Cake Mix in place of Fudge Marble Cake Mix. Divide dough as directed, then color one portion of dough with red or green food coloring.

BISCOTTI

1 (8-ounce) package PHILADELPHIA BRAND® Cream Cheese, softened
¾ cup PARKAY® Margarine, softened
¾ cup sugar
1 teaspoon vanilla
½ teaspoon anise extract
4 eggs
3¼ cups all-purpose flour
1 teaspoon CALUMET® Baking Powder
⅛ teaspoon salt
½ cup sliced almonds, toasted

Preheat oven to 400°F.

Beat cream cheese, margarine, sugar, vanilla and anise extract in large mixing bowl at medium speed with electric mixer until well blended. Blend in eggs.

Gradually add combined dry ingredients; mix well. Stir in almonds.

On well-floured surface with floured hands, shape dough into three 12×1½-inch logs. Place logs, 2 inches apart, on greased and floured cookie sheet.

Bake 15 to 20 minutes or until light golden brown. (Dough will spread and flatten slightly during baking.) Cool slightly.

Diagonally cut each log into ¾-inch slices. Place on cookie sheet.

Continue baking 5 to 10 minutes or until light golden brown. Cool on wire rack.

Makes about 3 dozen cookies

CHOCO-CARAMEL DELIGHTS

- ⅔ cup sugar
- ½ cup butter or margarine, softened
- 1 egg, separated
- 2 tablespoons milk
- 1 teaspoon vanilla extract
- 1 cup all-purpose flour
- ⅓ cup HERSHEY®S Cocoa
- ¼ teaspoon salt
- 1 cup finely chopped pecans
- Caramel Filling (recipe follows)
- ½ cup HERSHEY®S Semi-Sweet Chocolate Chips or Premium Semi-Sweet Chocolate Chunks
- 1 teaspoon shortening

In small mixer bowl, beat sugar, butter, egg yolk, milk and vanilla until blended. Stir together flour, cocoa and salt; blend into butter mixture. Chill dough at least 1 hour or until firm enough to handle.

Preheat oven to 350°F. Lightly grease cookie sheets. Beat egg white slightly. Shape dough into 1-inch balls. Dip each ball into egg white; roll in pecans to coat. Place 1 inch apart on prepared cookie sheet. Press thumb gently in center of each ball.

Bake 10 to 12 minutes or until set. While cookies bake, prepare Caramel Filling. Press center of each cookie again with thumb to make indentation. Immediately spoon about ½ teaspoon Caramel Filling in center of each cookie. Carefully remove to wire racks to cool completely.

In small microwave-safe bowl combine chocolate chips and shortening. Microwave at HIGH (100%) 1 minute or until softened; stir. Allow to stand several minutes to finish melting; stir until smooth. Place waxed paper under wire racks with cookies. Drizzle chocolate mixture over top of cookies.

Makes about 2 dozen cookies

Caramel Filling: In small saucepan, combine 14 unwrapped light caramels and 3 tablespoons whipping cream. Cook over low heat, stirring frequently, until caramels are melted and mixture is smooth.

Choco-Caramel Delights

OATS 'N' PUMPKIN PINWHEELS

1½ cups sugar, divided
½ cup (1 stick) margarine, softened
2 egg whites
1½ cups all-purpose flour
1 cup QUAKER® Oats (Quick or Old Fashioned, uncooked)
¼ teaspoon baking soda
1 cup canned pumpkin
½ teaspoon pumpkin pie spice
¼ cup sesame seeds

Beat 1 cup sugar and margarine until fluffy; mix in egg whites. Stir in combined flour, oats and baking soda. On waxed paper, press into 16×12-inch rectangle. Spread combined pumpkin, remaining ½ cup sugar and spice over dough to ½ inch from edge. From narrow end, roll up dough. Sprinkle sesame seeds around roll, pressing gently. Wrap in waxed paper; freeze overnight or until firm.

Preheat oven to 400°F. Spray cookie sheet with no-stick cooking spray. Cut frozen dough into ¼-inch slices; place 1 inch apart on prepared cookie sheet.

Bake 9 to 11 minutes or until golden brown. Remove to wire rack; cool completely. *Makes about 4 dozen cookies*

CHOCOLATE-DIPPED ALMOND CRESCENTS

One end of these crescent-shaped cookies is dipped into melted chocolate—a decorative touch that makes them look special.

1 cup butter or margarine, softened
1 cup powdered sugar
2 egg yolks
2½ cups all-purpose flour
1½ teaspoons almond extract
1 cup (6 ounces) semisweet chocolate chips

Preheat oven to 375°F. Line cookie sheets with parchment paper or leave ungreased. Cream butter, sugar and egg yolks in large bowl. Beat in flour and almond extract until well mixed. Shape dough into 1-inch balls. (If dough is too soft to handle, cover and refrigerate until firm.) Roll balls into 2-inch long ropes, tapering both ends. Curve ropes into crescent shapes. Place 2 inches apart on prepared cookie sheets.

Bake 8 to 10 minutes or until set, but not browned. Remove to wire racks to cool. Melt chocolate chips in top of double boiler over hot, not boiling, water. Dip one end of each crescent in melted chocolate. Place on waxed paper; cool until chocolate is set. *Makes about 5 dozen cookies*

Caramel Lace Chocolate Chip Cookies

CARAMEL LACE CHOCOLATE CHIP COOKIES

- ¼ BUTTER FLAVOR CRISCO® Stick or ¼ cup BUTTER FLAVOR CRISCO all-vegetable shortening
- ½ cup light corn syrup
- 1 tablespoon brown sugar
- ½ teaspoon vanilla
- 1½ teaspoons grated orange peel (optional)
- ½ cup all-purpose flour
- ¼ teaspoon salt
- ⅓ cup semi-sweet chocolate chips
- ⅓ cup coarsely chopped pecans

1. Preheat oven to 375°F. Grease baking sheet with shortening.

2. Combine shortening, corn syrup, brown sugar, vanilla and orange peel in large bowl. Beat at medium speed of electric mixer until well blended.

3. Combine flour and salt. Mix into creamed mixture at low speed until blended. Stir in chocolate chips and nuts. Drop teaspoonfuls of dough 4 inches apart onto baking sheet.

4. Bake 5 minutes or until edges are golden brown. (Chips and nuts will remain in center while dough spreads out.) *Do not overbake.* Cool 2 minutes on baking sheet. Lift cookie edge with edge of spatula. Grasp cookie edge gently and lightly pinch or flute the edge, bringing it up to the chips and nuts in center. Work around each cookie until completely fluted. Remove to cooling rack. *Makes about 3 dozen cookies*

Acknowledgments

FAVORITE BRAND NAME RECIPES MAGAZINE would like to thank the companies and organizations listed below for the use of their recipes in this magazine.

Almond Board of California
American Egg Board
Best Foods, a division of CPC International Inc.
Blue Diamond Growers
Borden Kitchens, Borden, Inc.
California Apricot Advisory Board
Diamond Walnut Growers, Inc.
Dole Food Company, Inc.
Domino Sugar Corporation
Florida Department of Citrus
Hershey Foods Corporation
Kahlúa Liqueur
Kraft Foods, Inc.
Leaf®, Inc.
M&M/Mars
Nestlé Food Company
Procter & Gamble Company
The Quaker Oats Company
USA Rice Council
Sokol and Company
Sun·Maid Growers of California
Walnut Marketing Board
Wisconsin Milk Marketing Board

Photo Credits

FAVORITE BRAND NAME RECIPES MAGAZINE would like to thank the companies and organizations listed below for the use of their photographs in this magazine.

Almond Board of California
Best Foods, a division of CPC International Inc.
Borden Kitchens, Borden, Inc.
California Apricot Advisory Board
Hershey Foods Corporation
Kraft Foods, Inc.
Leaf®, Inc.
Procter & Gamble Company
The Quaker Oats Company
USA Rice Council
Sokol and Company
Walnut Marketing Board
Wisconsin Milk Marketing Board

Index

METRIC CONVERSION CHART

VOLUME MEASUREMENTS (dry)

1/8 teaspoon = 0.5 mL
1/4 teaspoon = 1 mL
1/2 teaspoon = 2 mL
3/4 teaspoon = 4 mL
1 teaspoon = 5 mL
1 tablespoon = 15 mL
2 tablespoons = 30 mL
1/4 cup = 60 mL
1/3 cup = 75 mL
1/2 cup = 125 mL
2/3 cup = 150 mL
1/4 cup = 175 mL
1 cup = 250 mL
2 cups = 1 pint = 500 mL
3 cups = 750 mL
4 cups = 1 quart = 1 L

VOLUME MEASUREMENTS (fluid)

1 fluid ounce (2 tablespoons) = 30 mL
4 fluid ounces (1/2 cup) = 125 mL
8 fluid ounces (1 cup) = 250 mL
12 fluid ounces (1 1/2 cups) = 375 mL
16 fluid ounces (2 cups) = 500 mL

WEIGHTS (mass)

1/2 ounce = 15 g
1 ounce = 30 g
3 ounces = 90 g
4 ounces = 120 g
8 ounces = 225 g
10 ounces = 285 g
12 ounces = 360 g
16 ounces = 1 pound = 450 g

DIMENSIONS

1/16 inch = 2 mm
1/8 inch = 3 mm
1/4 inch = 6 mm
1/2 inch = 1.5 cm
3/4 inch = 2 cm
1 inch = 2.5 cm

OVEN TEMPERATURES

250°F = 120°C
275°F = 140°C
300°F = 150°C
325°F = 160°C
350°F = 180°C
375°F = 190°C
400°F = 200°C
425°F = 220°C
450°F = 230°C

BAKING PAN SIZES

Utensil	Size in Inches/Quarts	Metric Volume	Size in Centimeters
Baking or Cake Pan (square or rectangular)	8×8×2	2 L	20×20×5
	9×9×2	2.5 L	22×22×5
	12×8×2	3 L	30×20×5
	13×9×2	3.5 L	33×23×5
Loaf Pan	8×4×3	1.5 L	20×10×7
	9×5×3	2 L	23×13×7
Round Layer Cake Pan	8×1 1/2	1.2 L	20×4
	9×1 1/2	1.5 L	23×4
Pie Plate	8×1 1/4	750 mL	20×3
	9×1 1/4	1 L	23×3
Baking Dish or Casserole	1 quart	1 L	—
	1 1/2 quart	1.5 L	—
	2 quart	2 L	—

Bring back the memories and traditions of Christmas past by baking your own scrumptious *Christmas Cookies.*

31415
0 42799 31415 9
ISBN 0-7853-1415-6